"*We've all snatched defeat from the jaw* interview. *That's because when we don't rise to the occasion, we sink to the level of our preparation. No more. This is the best book I've seen to prepare thoroughly for any interview, and set yourself up for success.*"
— Michael Bungay Stanier, WSJ bestselling author

"*Finding the right employer-employee fit is so important, and yet so hard. Companies invest so much in recruiting, interviewing, and onboarding the right candidates, and the wrong fit is incredibly expensive. When candidates know what they want, and come in prepared with the right questions, the odds of a successful match increase considerably. This book is a must for candidates, hiring managers, and recruiters!*"
— Joanna McFarland, Co-Founder and CEO, HopSkipDrive

"*Many people are reactive in their careers and let inertia drive their path. At RevelOne, we've seen that the most successful executives are introspective about the types of skills they bring and proactively identify the companies where they can have the most impact. Ask Me This Instead gives candidates a blueprint for this type of thinking and will ultimately help them achieve their near and long-term career goals.*"
— Gary Calega, Co-Founder, RevelOn

Other Books Available at Holloway.com

The Holloway Guide to Remote Work
Katie Womersley, Juan Pablo Buriticá et al.

A comprehensive guide to building, managing, and adapting to working with distributed teams.

The Holloway Guide to Technical Recruiting and Hiring
Osman (Ozzie) Osman et al.

A practical, expert-reviewed guide to growing software engineering teams effectively, written by and for hiring managers, recruiters, interviewers, and candidates.

The Holloway Guide to Equity Compensation
Joshua Levy, Joe Wallin et al.

Stock options, RSUs, job offers, and taxes—a detailed reference, explained from the ground up.

The Holloway Guide to Raising Venture Capital
Andy Sparks et al.

A current and comprehensive resource for entrepreneurs, with technical detail, practical knowledge, real-world scenarios, and pitfalls to avoid.

Founding Sales: The Early-Stage Go-To-Market Handbook
Pete Kazanjy

This tactical handbook distills early sales first principles, and teaches the skills required for going from being a founder to early salesperson, and eventually becoming an early sales leader.

Angel Investing: Start to Finish
Joe Wallin, Pete Baltaxe

A journey through the perils and rewards of angel investing, from fundamentals to finding deals, financings, and term sheets.

Ask Me This Instead

Ask Me This Instead

FLIP THE INTERVIEW TO LAND YOUR DREAM JOB

Kendra Haberkorn

Why should only hiring managers and recruiters decide your job destiny? Be empowered at every step of the hiring process, understand your own skills and priorities, and find the company that can give you what you want. No matter where you are in your career journey, it's time you were in control.

RACHEL JEPSEN, EDITOR

HOLLOWAY

Copyright © 2020 Kendra Haberkorn
All rights reserved.

No part of this publication may be reproduced or transmitted in any form or by any means,
electronic or mechanical, including photocopying, recording, or any other information storage or
retrieval system, without prior permission in writing from the publisher.

This work and all associated content, such as online comments and discussion, do not
constitute legal or tax advice in any respect. No reader should act or refrain from acting on the
basis of any information presented here without seeking the advice of counsel in the relevant
jurisdiction. The contributors to this work may not be licensed in your jurisdiction. They and
Holloway, Inc. expressly disclaim all warranties or liability in respect of any actions taken or not
taken based on any contents or associated content.

Published in the United States by Holloway, San Francisco
Holloway.com

Cover design by Order (New York) and Andy Sparks
Interior design by Joshua Levy and Jennifer Durrant
Print engineering by Titus Wormer

Typefaces: Tiempos Text and National 2
by Kris Sowersby of Klim Type Foundry

Print version 1.0 · Digital version e1.0.0
doc 5b8e45 · pipeline 3fd04e · genbook edc257
2020-10-11

A Note from the Publisher

Holloway publishes books online. As a reader of this special full-access print edition, you are granted personal access to the paid digital edition, which you can read and share on the web, and offers commentary, updates, and corrections. A Holloway account also gives access to search, definitions of key terms, bookmarks, highlights, and other features. Claim your account by visiting: **holloway.com/print20268**

If you wish to recommend the book to others, suggest they visit **holloway.com/amti** to learn more and purchase their own digital or print copy.

The author welcomes your feedback! Please consider adding comments or suggestions to the book online so others can benefit. Or say hello@holloway.com. Thank you for reading.

The Holloway team

LEGEND

Some elements in the text are marked for special significance:

◇ IMPORTANT	Important or often overlooked tip
⚠ DANGER	Serious warning or pitfall where risks or costs are significant
▣ STORY	A personal anecdote or story

Web links appear as numbered footnotes in print.

References to other related sections are indicated by superscript section numbers, prefixed with §.

TABLE OF CONTENTS

1 Introduction

I have 15 years of experience interviewing thousands of people, expertise in designing interview processes, and I coach individuals as they search and interview for new jobs. I've read books, dissected online reviews and articles, consulted hiring managers and leaders in order to build a series of conversations that let teams hone in, assess, and hire the people they need and believe can do the job. I know a lot about interviewing.

And I'm going to tell you a secret. The most important questions asked in an interview process are those the candidate asks the interviewer—not the other way around.

Of course, this isn't the way we've been trained to think about interviewing. When you sit across the table from a hiring manager or prospective team member, you're focused on sharing your experience and skills in a way that convinces the interviewer that you're the right person for the job. While hiring teams are making a single decision—whether to move you to the next step—you are making *many* decisions throughout the process. Decisions that will change your career, and possibly your life. I wrote this book because I believe candidates can get a lot out of the interview process. Whether or not you receive an offer or decide this is the job for you, preparing for and ultimately sitting through the interview is an opportunity to think about yourself, what you can offer, and what you really want.

Throughout my career, I've done the job I was hired to do by creating systems, hiring criteria, question guides, and scorecards. Those tools, as well as the training and techniques behind them, were valuable. At the same time, I always felt like the hiring process was missing the mark in a major way. The interviewers, questions, and type of assessments are designed to help the team get a 360° view into a candidate's capabilities and potential to fulfill the responsibilities of the role. With the emphasis on designing to achieve the *company's* objectives, I rarely had the time, the directive, or the incentive to design for the candidate (aka, you, the person reading this book and preparing for upcoming interviews). I didn't have the chance to ask myself, what would make this process better for *you*? After all, what was best for you had benefits for the team and company as well. When both the individual and company get what they are looking for out of the process, there is an increased likelihood of success and satisfaction as well as the opportunity to proactively address any gaps before someone starts, setting the stage for a smooth onboarding process.

When I'm conducting the interview, I save time for a candidate to ask me questions. Several years ago, I realized that this portion of the interview felt like déjà vu; a significant portion of candidates, regardless of their discipline, seniority, background, or other factors, were asking me the *same* questions.

In return, I recited the same answers. My responses were true—I always wanted to give an authentic answer but the words were "canned." I didn't have to reflect on my experience or think critically about some aspect of the company to provide a compelling answer that was relevant to that candidate. I would customize or connect dots in some way, but the building blocks sections of my responses rolled off my tongue with ease.

I started to keep a document of the most common questions, particularly the ones I was most tired of answering. Every now and then, I'd open it and add to the list. Over the course of a couple of years, the list grew. Sometimes, I found myself wanting to intervene during those last few minutes of interviews. I would feel the urge to stop the conversation and share a few ideas about what I thought the candidate should ask to get the most out of our time together. After asking them questions for 30 minutes to an hour, I knew about their experience, motivations, strengths, and development opportunities, and had insight into the things that they might want to know, but hadn't thought to ask.

Most of the questions candidates did ask were so broad and generic that I responded in kind—saying what amounted to a lot of nothing. It bothered me. I was invested in the process. I wanted the team and their new hire to be successful. Yet, the interview process for many candidates barely broke the surface of the discovery and exploration that would have enabled the candidate to really dissect, digest, and determine if this was really the right opportunity for them. For candidates to have those revelations was in our best interest—the more we all knew about what the real working relationship and environment would amount to, the better off we'd all be. As a talent leader, I knew that the gaps in the interview process on either side were often the roots of the problems that would follow later.

As a team member, I also knew the dirt—the pain points and problems they were likely to encounter. I understood the organizational and interpersonal challenges that would emerge when the politeness of the interview and onboarding process faded away. I remembered the responsibilities that didn't make it into the job description. With my broad view into different departments, I had insight into the hidden aspects of the company and team. I wanted them to ask me about those things! To challenge me in order to uncover the real details of working at the company or for a particular manager. Then, if they had the chance to step into the role they wanted, they would do so with eyes wide open.

When those issues came up, or when someone left because the job or team didn't meet their expectations, I was often left thinking, "I wished you'd asked me *this* instead. I would have told you what you wanted to know."

I want you to get as much value out of the limited time available within the hiring process—to be able to explore the priorities and topics that will make a difference in *your* decision. And that's what this book will empower you to do. There are five sections to this book that will help you proactively plan for and adeptly navigate the interview process as you seek out and succeed in getting your next role.

- **Target Companies and Evaluate Roles.** In this section, I'll help you evaluate open roles and companies, interpret incoming information and available resources and start to prioritize and refine what really matters to you, right now. With this information, you can target your search, effectively prepare for interviews, and stand out relative to other candidates.
- **Write a Resume That Tells Your Career Story.** In this section, you'll create a stand-out resume that reflects your experience, your priorities, and where you want to go. Activities will help you identify the characters in your career story, map out pivotal moments, connect your story to a company's needs, write a cover letter, and much more.
- **People and Power in the Interview Process.** In this section, I'll break down the obvious participants and those who can play critical, if less visible, roles in determining whether or not you get the job. I'll provide you with insights to navigate these conversations and develop strong relationships. You'll learn how to target your questions to each specific

person to get the information you need, and make the right impression.

- **Ask Me This Instead.** In this section, you'll find the *Ask Me This Instead* question database, with over 100 questions that can be filtered by targeted interviewer and topic. I'll help you reframe typical questions that candidates ask interviewers to go deeper so that you get more honest, authentic, and unplanned answers. The more you can get beyond the canned, sales-pitch responses, the more you'll gain. Great questions will give you confidence. You'll learn why you shouldn't leave the "asking" up to the interviewers and how you can drive the process. In this section, you'll also complete an activity to help you design your interview game plan and keep track of what you learn.

- **Warning Signs in Interviews.** In this section, I'll highlight behind-the-scenes scenarios that could impact your hiring process and eventual experience on the job so that you can recognize and proactively address potential issues.

- **Developmental Career Strategy.** In this section, I'll make the case that the cycle of reflection and interviewing will help ensure you get the job you want now and the career you want in the long-term. I'll direct you to change the way you approach the job search from a time-bound and outcome-focused task to an ongoing, developmental career strategy. This proactive strategy will ensure you have options whenever you need or want a new job.

2 Target Companies and Evaluate Roles

At many points throughout our lives, we decide that it's time to find a new job and we begin to search, evaluate, and take steps to pursue specific companies and positions. The search often starts with Google or LinkedIn and a specific current or aspirational job title. There are geographic, industry or functional job boards that curate a more tailored list of roles and there are professional and personal networks too. Jobs and opportunities are more discoverable than ever. In fact, they find you! If you start searching online, you'll begin to see ads or postings pop up wherever you go. Then, if you look at recruiters representing a particular discipline or company, you might see their name pop up in your inbox asking to connect.

With so much information it should be easy to find the right opportunity. It's not, and that's not for lack of information or access.

The more information and choices you have in front of you, the harder it is to narrow your focus on the right opportunities. Pair information overload, inbound requests from recruiters, and jobs ads that find you with the sales and marketing messaging built into the recruiting process, and there is the chance that you'll end up applying to, interviewing for and accepting a job that sounded great all along but is not what you're interested in doing. I've seen this play out time and time again and even had it happen to me.

I thought that I was good at making decisions about my career. But as I reflected on the last couple of years, I realized I had trusted the companies and teams to do the evaluation for me. As they became more excited about my candidacy for their position and my ability to fit their needs, I became more excited. I ended up not asking the tough questions and did not orient my decision around the things that truly mattered most to me at that particular time in my life and career.

If you're reading this, there is a good chance you're looking for a new job or starting to interview with companies. Interviews are exciting, time-consuming, and stressful for many people. With the impact of the decisions resulting from these conversations, that's not surprising. A significant portion of the stress is tied to the end outcome. When we put ourselves out there and find a role or company where we can see ourselves working, succeeding, and thriving, we get attached to that future version of ourselves. We start to daydream about what the new role will do for our careers, bank account, and reputation. We begin to spend time reviewing our resume, pulling up old performance reviews ("What are my strengths, really?"), and practicing responses to interview questions in front of the mirror, on our commute, or with a trusted friend or family member. As the process progresses, so does the investment we're making in that outcome. We might start telling our friends, shopping for a new work wardrobe, even apartment hunting.

◇ IMPORTANT The cost (personal, financial and otherwise) of accepting the wrong job is high. And, the prospect of finding a new job is daunting. We shouldn't have to rely on other people's excitement or on our own imperfect instincts—with all our blind spots and gaps in self-awareness—when making choices in our careers. Luckily, with thoughtful and diligent preparation, you won't have to, and the entire process will be more manageable and productive. My preparation strategy will take you through a variety of specific activities and actions that build upon one another.

You'll begin by reflecting on and designating your top priorities[§2.1] for your next role. Then, you'll research roles that align with your priorities, starting with those titles and positions you're most familiar with.

Next, you'll broaden your search through an activity that will enable you to find roles[§2.16] with unexpected or unique titles that are tied to your priorities, so that you understand the full landscape of opportunities you can pursue.

Moving beyond research, you'll analyze the job descriptions[§2.18] to determine which roles and companies most closely match your objectives and excite you.

Once you are familiar with the opportunities, you'll work through a chapter and some exercises that will help you tell your career story, refine your resume, and solidify or update your priorities[§3] before you apply.

Together, these activities will help you understand how your past experiences, interests, and aspirations are connected. You'll reconfirm the type of environments and teams that led to your most fulfilling, fun, rewarding work, as well as those experiences that you'd prefer not to encounter again. With this preparation as the foundation, you'll be ready to articulate your accomplishments throughout the interviews and have a targeted list of questions you'll want the interviewer to answer.

2.1 *Determine Your Job Priorities*

You can't optimize for everything. It is incredibly rare for a particular job to meet or exceed all of your expectations. There are many aspects of the work experience that you will have to understand and evaluate while you are looking for a new job. Some, such as the role, your pay and benefits, and the people you'll collaborate with on a daily basis, are easy to connect to your personal experience right away. Others, including broader company context and long-term career opportunities, may not be as tangible from the start, but may be among the most important criteria for you.

As you pursue the application and interview process, you will receive a lot of information about each of these topics. Most of the time, the messages will be subtle and embedded into a larger conversation. This is why a clear understanding of what you want to prioritize will enable you to proactively listen for signals and ask specific questions to get a comprehensive picture of how a particular opportunity aligns with what matters most to you. When your core priorities and actual work experience complement one another, you can focus on your achievement and fulfillment. However, if aspects of your work experience don't match the factors you know are most important to your satisfaction and success, problems will emerge. Initially, the problems might be subtle frustrations. Over time, those annoyances will build and the cumulative impact of an ongoing, growing issue can become intolerable.

As you read through the priorities outlined in this section, reflect on your past experiences and take the time to complete the activity, Rank Your Top Priorities.$^{\S2.14}$ By doing so, you'll have clarity about what priorities you should focus on as you interview for jobs. Later, in the Ask Me This Instead^{§5} section, you'll have the chance to select questions tied to your priorities that will help you get to the heart of these matters in each of your conversations.

2.2 *Role*

The combination of responsibilities and expectations that fill your days at work are what constitute the role. For many people, the role is, without a doubt, one of their top priorities in the job search. Choosing to focus on the tangible foundation of what work represents, particularly as we spend many hours of most days focused on those activities, makes sense.

So, what are the indicators that the role might be one of your top priorities?

- This role is a critical stepping stone on a longer-term career path.
- You are pursuing an educational certificate, degree, or training program to gain access to a specific type of role (e.g. a coding bootcamp, MBA or apprenticeship program).
- The position represents a meaningful promotion or acceleration of your professional trajectory.

- The way you spend your days—the activities, tools and interactions—is key to your satisfaction, productivity, or fulfillment.
- You are making an intentional shift or pivot in a new direction.

If the bullets above resonate, focus on the following aspects of the role in your interview preparation and conversations.

First, people often think the job description is an accurate representation of the role. I'll go into more details about job descriptions later,[§2.18] but for now, know that they are not as indicative of the work or experience as they should be. You will need to push to get a real, tangible view into what the day-to-day looks like. For example, it's incredibly helpful to understand which meetings you will attend, the cadence of deadlines and how much of your time is spent in various activities. You'll want to make sure the team can articulate these elements of the job in more depth than what is on the job description. You'll need to ask them to show you the day-to-day experience via a glimpse into weekly calendars, reviewing agendas or letting you audit meetings. The title section of this book, Ask Me This Instead,[§5] will help you develop a list of questions to do this! If you don't know what you'll actually be doing, it's hard to know if you'll enjoy it or be successful.

◇ IMPORTANT Job responsibilities are distinct from expectations, though they often get bundled together. To understand the role, you need to get clarity on the responsibilities as well as the expectations. Responsibilities are the tasks, activities, and meetings that fill your day. Expectations are the more subtle measures of success, the "how" you get the work done, the way the team wants you to show up. You could be an expert in the execution of the tasks and still not meet expectations.

Responsibilities may be metrics—quantifiable, demonstrable outcomes you need to achieve or projects and documents you need to deliver. While there might be subjectivity associated with the approach, quality, value, or impact when it comes to responsibilities, there is also a binary element that is more easy to discern. Did you reach the target numbers or submit the report on time or not?

You often find out there was an expectation when you fail to meet it. It's the nuance—the unsaid beliefs about what really matters that will ultimately shape your experience and how people perceive your performance. These underlying expectations might include whether you answer emails or Slacks "on time," whether you work "enough" hours, whether your attitude and presence in meetings "mesh" with the team's, or whether you adeptly navigate office politics without ruffling feathers. The quotes are intentional. Most of the time, leaders know what they mean when they say "on time," "enough," and "mesh," but they don't communicate their expectations properly. It's frustrating and can be the result of intentional manipulation or poor management. Either way, it's hard to recover.

Your references can also be extremely helpful when evaluating a role and throughout the rest of the interview process. While preparing your application, ask them to review the job description and highlight examples of why they think you'll be a strong candidate (or if they think it's not the right next move). They will likely share insights and examples that you wouldn't have come up with otherwise. It's also possible that they'll point out areas where you will need to grow and learn to fulfill the responsibilities of the position. These tips can help you proactively consider a learning plan and prioritize where you might want to proactively prepare to address questions that will come your way during interviews. The added bonus of this exercise? You're prepping your references to have examples ready to share with hiring managers or recruiters as you get to the final stages of the process!

Spend extra effort on the questions database§5 later in the book to hone in on getting the answers you need to these questions! If you know the responsibilities, understand the expectations and are excited to step in, work hard and live up to all those "asks," your success will follow.

2.3 *Inclusion and Belonging*

Many companies are focusing more on diversity, equity, inclusion, and belonging. For individuals, the existence or absence of a feeling of belonging can transform their work experience, performance, and satisfaction. When you *belong*, and when you can show up as your authentic self, you are more likely to not only survive at work, but thrive. An exclusionary environment, one that denies you the opportunity to be yourself, or expects you to withhold certain parts of yourself, can chip away at your confidence, relationships, and commitment in meaningful and often painful ways. We all want to be accepted for who we are, including those aspects of our identity that are visible as well as those parts of ourselves that we hold more closely or that are not visible.

◇ IMPORTANT This conversation is evolving, and thankfully, becoming one that is top of mind for leaders and businesses everywhere. As this book is being written, dynamic discussions and debates are influencing the "what", "when" and "how," but also the "who" and "why" for initiatives and actions tied to diversity, equity, inclusion, and belonging. The language and priorities are shifting while leaders react, respond, and commit to a path forward. In this section and throughout the book, I'll use the abbreviation DEI for diversity, equity, and inclusion. Belonging and justice are part of the equation, though not as familiar as part of an acronym at this time. On the note of acronyms and language, different terms are used or preferred in different contexts and awareness about the nuance and significance of these terms is beneficial (find out more about exclusionary words you might come across in the hiring process here[1] and culturally conscious identifiers here[2]). The landscape will change by tomorrow and your own perspective may be very different from that which is presented here or elsewhere—and that's the point! As you approach your career and find the opportunities that are right for you, your own experience and opinions and how they relate to the company and team you're considering joining, matter.

In a contrived structure like a hiring process, it can be difficult to know when to bring your full self into the conversation and to anticipate how others will respond to what is uniquely you. Though the topic is nuanced and conversations can be difficult to initiate, it is important that you realize you have permission to ask questions and advocate for yourself. Before you'd make a decision about accepting a role, you need to understand whether or not the work environment will build you up or break you down. Your happiness and health, not to mention your success, will depend on it.

For some, belonging is not something that is a conscious, daily effort. Perhaps you've always felt like you belonged at work, or have been part of the majority and never had an experience where you were excluded or treated differently because of who you are. If this is you, this section

---

1. https://blog.ongig.com/writing-job-descriptions/
   a-list-of-offensive-exclusionary-words-used-in-job-descriptions/
2. https://www.prnewsonline.com/identifiers-emojis-diversity

is as important for you as it is for those who have had dramatically different experiences. Gaining empathy and understanding about the lives of others is valuable as the implications of these realizations about your similarities and differences can have meaningful impacts on your work and life experience. As we become more connected and spend more time at work and with our colleagues, the need for community and belonging has become more present, visible, and urgent. Understanding whether or not this potential work environment values diversity and takes tangible steps to bring everyone along can be a key decision criteria as you think about how the work environment and team will shape you, your experience and knowledge, and your understanding of the world around you. Diversity in leadership significantly improves a company's chances of success,[3] in startups[4] and established companies, and contributes toward the long-term culture and experience of the team as well.

There are many people, and perhaps even you, who know first hand the impact of being the only team member who is a person of color, who has a disability, who is LGBTQIA+, from a particular generation or the only woman in a room. For individuals who claim one or more of these identities or who bring yet another point of view and lived experience onto the team, a desire for belonging, as well as physical and psychological safety, are an omnipresent reality and priority. On top of the day-to-day stress of work, people with these visible or unseen aspects of identity are also subject to more microaggressions, discrimination, harassment, and violence.

No one wants to inadvertently join a company where they, or other team members, will be subject to unacceptable treatment and a lack of respect for their humanity. If we all seek out and demand environments that prioritize DEI, teams will become more representative, we'll see the benefit of increasing innovation, and both businesses and individuals will thrive.

If you want to…

- show up as your authentic self without having to assimilate, code switch, change or adjust parts of yourself;

---

3. https://www.mckinsey.com/featured-insights/diversity-and-inclusion/
diversity-wins-how-inclusion-matters
4. https://www.holloway.com/g/venture-capital/sections/
bias-and-discrimination-in-fundraising

- work with team members who will embrace and respect your experiences (*even if they do not or cannot understand them!*), bring you along, and amplify your voice and talent; and
- work for a company that supports the values, social movements and causes you believe in

...then take a proactive approach to understand how a company and team support diversity, equity, inclusion, and belonging in the following dimensions.

2.3.1 EVALUATE THE COMPANY'S EFFORTS

Are a company's efforts integral and genuine, or superficial and performative? As you research, prepare questions to ask your interviewers, and go through conversations, you will need to probe into the details about the company's philosophy and tangible actions to understand where a particular organization and team are on their DEI journey.

- Are the company's efforts proactive—taking steps toward a more inclusive environment on an ongoing basis—or reactive—responding to issues or pressure only when they arise?
- Does the company make statements or social posts but neglect to take specific internal actions that would lead to measurable change?
- Do different team members, and specifically those in leadership positions, share contrary or inconsistent information about what the company believes or does to support diversity, equity, inclusion, and belonging?
- Does the topic come up frequently on their website, in external press or profiles, in job descriptions and interviews, or only if you ask questions about it?

A company where this work is integral to the business and their values will be well-poised to respond to the events happening in the world. Companies in this position can proactively adapt their employee experience and culture while referencing and improving existing programs and practices. These companies will have existing infrastructure that enable them to support employees, and to take timely, thoughtful, and genuine action—whether a statement, donation, or policy change—in a consistent and sustainable manner. The response to these actions (e.g. on review sites like Glassdoor or in comments below the social or blog posts) from current and former employees will demonstrate enthusiasm and support for the efforts.

On the other hand, if a company's commitment is superficial or performative, you'll see spotty or inconsistent responses to the events impacting the world or members of their team. An email, social post or statement might be released without the underlying structures or support to drive real, tangible change. In other cases, companies may quickly join a viral social trend without fully understanding the origins[5] of the post or the implications of their use of a hashtag, as was apparent during the summer of 2020 when black squares filled social feeds and #BlackoutTuesday[6] began to trend and disrupt the actual goals of the campaign. A superficial approach is one that may have good intentions accompanied by a lack of follow-through and the absence of resources, time, money, and dedicated roles to support the effort. Performative displays or actions are often for the sake of optics or attention and to get through a moment, rather than support a movement. It is hard for companies to respond to every local, national, or international cause with the same level of attention or action. The absence of a response in a particular situation might be grounded in a targeted strategy of supporting a specific type of cause or a preference for behind-the-scenes donations, among many other possible scenarios. As you explore, remember that things are usually more complicated than they appear.

2.3.2 EVALUATE THE COMPANY'S TRACK RECORD AND ROADMAP

At the foundation, DEI work exists because individuals and leaders want to create and sustain positive change. To envision and create purposeful programs is difficult. To implement, maintain, and improve them is even more challenging. Some companies might be new to this work and "all in"; others have been at it for years and have barely tapped the surface of what is possible or necessary to make their workplace more representative, equitable, and inclusive.

Understanding where a company is coming from, as well as the plan for what they will do in the months or years that follow will illuminate aspects of their intentions and dedication to these efforts. To get to these

---

5. https://www.huffpost.com/entry/social-media-trend-questions_l_5edecbe0c5b66265393882ac

6. https://www.vox.com/the-goods/2020/6/3/21279336/blackout-tuesday-black-lives-matter-instagram-performative-allyship

insights, ask questions during your interviews that will help you examine the following:

- Does the company have programs or existing metrics and data available that highlight the work that has been done and indicates a sustained, ongoing commitment to future endeavors?
- Even if you would take a different approach, choose another way of framing or start with another initiative, do you feel comfortable and aligned with the progress, tactics and momentum you discover?
- Does the company have a prioritization or decision-making structure in place to determine which specific issues or opportunities they will address in their DEI efforts? Can the interviewers speak to how DEI efforts are chosen or sequenced? For example, is the team going to focus first on internal training programs about unconscious bias or update their recruiting process to be more inclusive?
- Are you able to find information about their partnerships, advertising spend, or investors to evaluate if there is consistency on the implied or stated values with that data or those decisions and outcomes?
- Can interviewers provide information about progress *and* failures in order to demonstrate an iterative and learning-focused approach to DEI efforts?

No company has a perfect track record and there isn't a formula for the roadmap of activities, investment, or changes to create a diverse, equitable, and inclusive workplace. Each company's strengths and opportunities will be unique given the evolving needs of their workforce. This is true even within a company. Individuals on the same team or with the same title might have dramatically different experiences, relationships, and outcomes. It's also true that departments or teams may have location-specific challenges based on the unique attributes of their environment and population. A one-size-fits-all approach is not sufficient, and could do more damage than good.

The process that a company uses to determine what investment and activities they dedicate time toward can indicate if they intend to solve the obvious or underlying problems as well as if they know who to bring into the conversation and how to make progress. Finding out what gets measured in surveys or employee data and how it gets presented to the team will also reinforce or invalidate the messages you hear throughout the hiring process.

As you go through the hiring process, from application through interviews and offer negotiations, ask revealing questions (the Ask Me This Instead section[§5] will equip you with some good ones!) and listen. In companies where this work is integral, you'll hear evidence and find examples of momentum and also come across reflection and humility around the missteps and failures. There should be both. No journey is without detours and roadblocks and these insights will help you choose whether or not this is the place where you will want to contribute your energy, expertise, and experience.

2.3.3 DETERMINE IF YOU WANT TO AND CAN BE PART OF THE JOURNEY

◇ IMPORTANT Once you understand where a company is at, as well as where it is going, you may choose to see how you can be involved. Or not. You may care deeply about how DEI manifests at an organization and choose not to invest your personal attention, emotional labor, and action to the work. It's also possible that you'll decide to weave in and out depending on where you are at work and in life and what you want to dedicate your energy to in that period. For some, this results in feelings of guilt or the perception that others are judging you for your choices. Stay true to your purpose and choose your commitments—this is work you can contribute to if you want to. Underrepresented individuals or groups should not do all the work—it must be an opt-in, remunerated effort that is collaborative with allies.

Regardless of how you may choose to participate, it is helpful to be aware of what the team, committee, or related community structures look like at a particular company. Select questions that will help you understand the answers to the following as you move through the interview process.

- Is this an "initiative" vs. a commitment or ongoing business priority?
- Is this a HR program? Does the work depend on or sit solely within that function? This is important because the role of a HR team as it supports the business and mitigates risk may conflict with the interests of those trying to transform the team and experience with regard to DEI from the inside. It's valuable to have someone in a leadership position who can partner with HR while advocating for these initiatives from a different perspective.
- Does it have the support of the CEO and other C-level leadership?
- Are the efforts tied to one person or a small group of people?

- Does the company have employee resource groups (ERGs), affinity organizations, or similar groups in place? What is the frequency and nature of their interactions? What programs are in motion and how are they progressing? What budget do they have to work with? Do the groups have organizational support?
- Does the company have a team or role dedicated to this work or is it something individuals do above and beyond their jobs?
- Do you have information that there is empowerment *and* support (e.g. budget) for those who participate?
- Are those involved open to new and even contrary points of view and will they respond to conflict and debate productively?
- How do participants feel their contributions are viewed and valued?

If you decide to dedicate your time and effort to this work, you'll want to know what you're getting into and how it will complement or contrast with other aspects of your role and experience. If the work belongs to a certain team, or if there is a dedicated role, there may be a particular focus and limits to what you can influence or contribute. In other instances, companies will have grassroots efforts, where anyone can contribute (likely in a volunteer capacity) and help shape the agenda, but your resources may be limited and your contributions may not be viewed with the same weight or impact as those critical to your role. Be aware that in some companies, if your participation in DEI efforts is viewed as distracting from your contributions in your role, or if you are viewed as part of the push for change, it may undermine how your job performance is viewed.

You'll have to make choices as you learn more in the interview process and once you've joined a company. As with other aspects of work, it's unlikely you'll find everything you're looking for. By asking questions and exploring how the companies you interview with are approaching this work, you're demonstrating the importance of these efforts. If every candidate asked about DEI in their interviews, the expectations and accountability to have a point of view and tangible evidence of a commitment would be reinforced. When you do this work and ask these questions, you're helping to pave the way for the team members and candidates who will follow. If this is something that matters to you, ask every interviewer a question about it. What they say, or what they are unable to share, will tell you everything.

In working on this section, and on broader, related themes throughout the book, I partnered with Megan Abman, Karyn Lu, and Regina Motarjeme from Strata RMK Consulting[7] to help expand my perspectives beyond the work environments I've been closest to in my career. With their deep passion, innate curiosity, data-driven and human-centric approach, the Strata team consults, educates, and leads teams and companies toward a resilient foundation and enduring commitment to diversity, equity, and inclusion. I am grateful for their partnership and wisdom and inspired by their work.

2.4 *People*

There is a reason why "people are our greatest asset" or "the people are the best thing about working here" are quotes you often hear about the work experience. Who we spend our long days with, and how we interact, communicate and collaborate with them, are meaningful elements of our jobs. Later in the book,[§4] we'll take a deep dive on specific people you're likely to meet in the interview process to help you think through the importance of different relationships. This section will focus on a broader spectrum of relationship-oriented criteria, including team dynamics and leadership influence.

How do you know if people, and specifically the team dynamics and leadership influence tied to those relationships, are one of your top priorities?

- You value and emphasize work relationships over work responsibilities.

---

7. https://strata-rmk.com/

- Work is a primary source of connection and community in your life.
- You prefer collaborative and interactive work environments and activities over solo, independent efforts.
- This is a network-building stage of your career that will help unlock doors in the future.

If relationships are one of your top priorities, make sure you get to know your interviewers! Throughout the interviews, you'll get information from and about them that you will be able to logically analyze. You'll also gain insights that will lead you to form intuitive impressions about each person and the group as a collective. It's unlikely that you'll be able to meet with every single person who works at the company, so these interviewers are also a proxy for the full team. If you believe that meeting with someone in a particular role or on a specific team would be critical to your ability to make a decision about joining the team, ask to have that conversation if the opportunity isn't offered.

Interviewers are unlikely to dish on the drama or politics, so let's explore how you get more information about the team dynamics. When you meet with people one on one, it's hard to judge how collaboration comes to life on a team and at a company. Yet, understanding individual perspectives as well as what the collective interaction looks like is key to the work experience.

> **STORY** I recall a team that I was part of where, if you met each of us individually, you might have been impressed by our qualifications. We would have appeared to be smart, capable, passionate individuals who could thoughtfully articulate elements of the business, a role's value proposition, and engage in a responsive, credible and personal way. At the same time, if you had observed all of us in a team meeting discussing a complicated or controversial decision, the differences in our styles and approaches would have been apparent. It's not that we didn't respect one another, or recognize each other's expertise, we just didn't have an effective approach to collaboration. We hadn't found our rhythm or invested in making the outcomes, as well as the journey to getting there together, more enjoyable.

To narrow the focus on what aspects of the team dynamics you will want to examine, focus on these four "Cs": communication, collaboration, competition, and community.

- **Communication.** How you like to share and receive updates

  - What are the methods or tools you find most effective when communicating with team members?
  - How frequently do you want or need to be in touch with others on your team?
  - How do you like to participate in or receive updates about important decisions?

- **Collaboration.** How you like to work with others on your team

  - Do you prefer group or independent work?
  - What makes collaborative meetings or activities most effective or enjoyable for you?
  - Do you like clear roles and responsibilities or a more open and evolving structure to projects?
  - Do you want to start a meeting with a detailed agenda or blank whiteboard?

- **Competition.** How you view individual and collective achievement

  - Are you motivated to ascend and focused on your own outcomes?
  - Do you enjoy roles or teams where individual performance drives rewards?
  - Are you comfortable with a hierarchy that impacts how people interact?

- **Community.** How you view your colleagues

  - Are you looking for interaction beyond and outside the workplace?
  - Do you see team members as prospective friends or prefer to keep your personal and professional lives separate?

It would be incredibly valuable if you could spend the day with a prospective team member shadowing meetings, observing the tools and technology that facilitates their work and gathering information about the pace and intensity of the role. Unfortunately, that experience is rare. Toward the end of the interview process, or after an offer, you can request the opportunity to audit a team meeting or follow a team member for all or a portion of one of their days. It's possible the company will give you the chance, which could meaningfully impact your understanding and perception about the role. If you get the chance to see a day in the life, take advantage of the opportunity to observe and ask more detailed questions! If not, leveraging the strategies outlined throughout this book will get you as close to an insider's view as possible.

Next, let's look at leadership. Whether you report to someone in the C-Suite or are starting out at the entry level, the influence of the leadership team will contribute to your experience. There are many types of leaders that you'll encounter along the way. Understanding what you value in their experience and approach will enable you to ascertain whether or not the company's leadership is what you're looking for in your next role.

In order to evaluate or probe in a relevant direction with your inter-viewers about the influence of leadership, take some time to consider the profiles of leaders you've worked with in the past. Identify the aspects of their approach that you admired and want to see replicated in future lead-ers and pinpoint the styles of leadership that will not support your current career objectives.

Here is a list of reflection questions to help you define what you're looking for from leadership as you refine your list of priorities:

- Do you value a leader's previous experience and prefer to work with those individuals who have solved similar problems in previous roles? Or, can you get excited about someone who has ascended into the lead-ership position quickly based on their intellect, ideas or expertise?
- Do you want the leadership team to have breadth and depth of experi-ence or are you comfortable with a team that has a narrow focus and set of expertise from a functional or industry point of view?
- Would you like to have leaders who lead from afar, trusting their teams to fulfill their roles, or are you someone who values a hands-on, involved leader?
- What about various leaders' communication styles did you appreciate in the past? What types of communication—or lack thereof—frus-trated you and impeded your success?
- Would you prefer your leader trust best practices and industry stan-dards or lean on experimentation, testing and exploration?

You will have to determine what styles of leadership resonate with you. This is particularly important for those you'll interact with the most—your manager—as well as those who will indirectly impact your experience from the top (like you're manager's manager). In conversations with your prospective manager,[§4.2] department executive[§4.3] and peers,[§4.7] listen for clues and ask specific questions[§5] to get more clarity on what leadership looks like at the company.

In evaluating the people aspect of a prospective opportunity, pay close attention to the words your interviewers say (as well as what they might leave out), their body language, inability or unwillingness to address certain topics, or a lack of enthusiasm and attention paid to the conversation overall. Monitor your reactions as well, specifically those that might yield insights that you will need to look into further. Take notes after the conversations about what you liked about the interaction and how you think it will contribute to a positive work experience. If you have lingering questions, add comments about what you might need to explore further with a particular member of the team. These reactions are fleeting but telling. Capturing reflections soon after the conversation so you can follow-up is worthwhile, especially if you are interviewing at multiple companies where experiences have the tendency to blend together. As you respond to interviewers' questions and listen to their responses to yours, assess whether or not you believe they are genuine and telling the truth.

Your goal is to find people who you will be able to collaborate with effectively; learn from and potentially teach things to; and who you can communicate with productively in order to accomplish required objectives. At certain stages of your career, you might be looking for even more out of these working relationships, for example, some team members eventually become dear friends. Knowing what you want out of these relationships and approaching the conversations with those priorities in mind will help you determine if you can see yourself in the team room, pushing toward deadlines and celebrating big wins with this particular group. As I stated above, in People and Power in the Interview Process,[§4] we'll dive deep into the specific people you're likely to meet to help you understand more about how they could influence your interview or working experience. The titular section, Ask Me This Instead,[§5] also includes questions for each of the core profiles so that you take advantage of the opportunity to understand their particular points of view on the topics that matter most to you.

2.5 *Offer Package*

The components and value of the offer package—the salary, benefits, bonus program, stock options, vacation time, volunteer opportunities, and more—are parts of the work experience that most people can't ignore. These are the factors that help us determine whether a particular job will enable us to live our lives. What you focus on within the offer package is highly dependent on your needs and desires.

Within the key aspects of an offer package, you might prioritize with the following in mind:

- Are you responsible for financially supporting yourself and/or others?
- Are focused on specific financial goals or obligations?
- Are health and wellbeing priorities for you, or for those you support?
- Do you want to balance the short vs. long-term rewards?
- Do you prefer stability and consistency or can you tolerate variability and risk?
- Is it important to you that the company provide volunteer days, donation matching, or other ways to support causes you believe in?

An entire book can be written about the offer and negotiation process.[8] This is not one of those books, but highlighting this component of the employment experience as an important aspect of what you need to reflect upon to codify your personal priorities and address during the hiring process is worthwhile. There are a few areas I want to emphasize as you prepare to interview and ask focused questions.§5

In recent years, the conversation has shifted and new laws have emerged to address pay inequity.[9] As someone who has talked to thousands of people about salary and seen offers and payroll files, I am glad there are great minds, brave voices, and admirable organizations working to address these gaps—because there is a lot of work left to do. Each of us can contribute to a more equitable future if we take steps to ask informed questions and gather inputs from credible sources that will help us advocate confidently to earn what our work is worth. And, by taking these steps for yourself, you pave the way for others like you. Some companies have taken bold steps to address the issues, adjust pay, and even publish

---

8. https://www.lewis-lin.com/salary-negotiation-emails-book
9. https://timesupfoundation.org/work/times-up-pay-up/
   gender-and-racial-inequity-during-crisis-the-pay-gap/

the salaries of all their employees[10] in an abundance of transparency, but most have not.

State and national laws, guidelines, and regulations vary[11] about when, if, and how employers can ask about or share information regarding pay, benefits, and other elements of an offer. These may be dependent on the level of a role. For example, executives may have access to different types of compensation or contracts outlining what they are entitled to throughout and at the conclusion of their employment. In other cases, there may be a union that negotiates on behalf of everyone. Pay is an important (OK, absolutely critical) aspect of employment for most people, and it's also very personal. What defines a satisfactory salary or hourly rate will depend on the person, their experience, the role and location, as well as their perception of the value of the contributions they make and the personal responsibilities they have to manage.

How can you take steps to get the rewards you deserve? First, start with publicly available information on various websites (including Salary.com, PayScale and Glassdoor) that highlight salary information for roles and by geography or other criteria. Consider this information directional. The inputs used to generate the average ranges are often anonymous, which means they may be accurate (after all, there isn't a motivation to misrepresent) but they are absent of meaningful context used to determine pay rates. For example, it can be hard to decipher the size of an organization, the breadth of the pay band (is that salary at the top end or bottom for that company and role), whether or not that person is a top performer or barely scraping by, if they've had raises and progression tied to market or individual results, and if their offer was determined or influenced by their past salaries,[12] experience, or other factors. Take these numbers and start to formulate your floor, the base level of a yearly salary or hourly wage that you'd be able (and ideally excited) to accept. Do your best to make that floor a realistic, achievable one for the roles you're targeting.

Once you have your target number or range—one that will cover your bills, enable you to save and enjoy life, and that will motivate you—I recommend you check it with a neutral and informed person (yes, a human being, not a website). Ask a recruiter or HR colleague from a former employer, or a former manager, peer, or executive who has visibility into

10. https://buffer.com/resources/salary-formula-changes-2019/

11. https://www.hrdive.com/news/salary-history-ban-states-list/516662/

12. https://hbr.org/2020/07/stop-asking-job-candidates-for-their-salary-history

recruiting and or internal pay bands in the field or function. You'll need to describe the role and responsibilities and the company size and stage to help them frame their response. Share an open range and ask them if they believe it's on point. This information and framing enables them to give you a more targeted and honest answer. They may adjust the range up or down or share other considerations that will help you feel more confident or lead you to do more research.

◇ IMPORTANT A lot of people won't take the steps to vet their compensation expectations. They'll make the determination on their own or with a close friend, partner, or spouse, because it can be awkward to talk about compensation. That's why it's so important. The more we talk about it, the better prepared and informed we'll all be. We won't have to wonder where we stand or if we could have asked for more. The more we talk about it, the less awkward it becomes, the more comfortable you'll be in conversations with hiring managers or recruiters about the salary of a job you want.

It's important to remember that base pay is not the only factor that matters in the offer. There are also benefit programs, paid time off or vacation time, parental leave, bonuses, stock awards, and other components that some companies will be able to offer their employees. The collective aspects of an offer, often called "compensation" or "total rewards," matter, and individual pieces will rank in a different order for different people. For example, if you have planned or ongoing health care needs, or if you are providing health care for a spouse or dependent, you will want to look at your current health insurance offering. What does it cost you each pay period or month; how much do you spend toward prescriptions, office visits, or other healthcare obligations; do you like the way the plan and access to providers is structured? If you plan to start a family in the next few years, you'll want to get an idea of what parental leave, childcare, and flexible schedule options are available.

As you kick off your job search, research what companies you're interested in offer across their different benefit programs—many have highlights listed on their careers page. Google unfamiliar terms or reach back out to the recruiter or HR professional in your network to get more information about anticipated costs and how these programs are implemented. Then, if you receive an offer, take the time to read up about their programs and policies and look into the associated eligibility and costs. If you have questions, or want more information, ask for it![§5] An informed decision is in your best interest and, while you may or may not be able to negotiate for everything you want, you will be able to put the advantages and tradeoffs of an offer into perspective.

2.6 *Work-Life Balance*

Work, whether we want it to or not, often crosses over and impacts the rest of our life. Understanding how a prospective opportunity complements or disrupts your personal priorities and interests is necessary. The language and conversation around "work-life balance" is evolving. Depending on the path you pursue and your personal preferences, how work plays into the rest of your life—and vise versa—varies significantly. It's also likely that what "balance" means to you will change throughout your career. At its core, work-life balance is about whether or not this particular role provides the space and flexibility for you to enjoy your life outside the office or bring parts of yourself *into* the office, for example, establishing friendships, celebrating holidays and heritage months, or sharing more about your weekends than commentary about the weather. Because I touch on relationships, community, and inclusion in the people,[§2.4] employee experience,[§2.13] and inclusion belonging[§2.3] sections, I'll hone in on schedules, boundaries, and how to evaluate the time commitment you're willing to give to a role.

What signals in your personal life might indicate that you'd want to focus on work-life balance in your next opportunity?

- You have personal or family obligations.
- External hobbies, passions or activities are important to you.
- Work is just that—work, and you want to be able to compartmentalize and contain its impact on the rest of your life.
- You are at a stage of your career where more time spent at work will pay off—perhaps because you believe in the mission or are working toward a promotion.
- You're coming off a period of intensity and want the pendulum to swing back toward balance.
- A remote role or flexible schedule will enable you to manage your work and personal commitments more effectively.

As your life changes, your priorities will change too. It's important to note that you can ask questions[§5] to clarify your understanding of a particular company's approach to balance without disclosing details about your "why" if you prefer to keep your personal life and considerations more private.

One of the most important places to start is tied to the schedule and hours you're required or expected to work. Some roles, depending on their classification, will have specific schedules and will be eligible for overtime. Often, there is more clarity with those positions about when you work, when you're off, and what responsibilities you have. For other roles, including those that do not have specific shifts, assigned schedules, or the need to track your time to calculate overtime pay, you'll have to spend more time figuring out what the real "schedule" is. While the reference to a 9-to-5 is common, the reality is that many people work many more hours than the so-called 40 hour work week. Sometimes, you'll see these signals in the job descriptions ("work hard/play hard," "you want to work *hard* on the *toughest* problems," "our team chooses to go above and beyond....always," "we do more, with less") or in Glassdoor reviews, but other times you'll have to push for answers.

Sometimes these extra hours are pushes to get key projects across the line, and staying late or coming early is manageable. In other scenarios, the role, team or even company consistently and continuously operate at a pace and intensity that requires long hours 5, 6 or even 7 days a week. Because work is on our phones, as well as in the office or on a laptop at many companies, the boundary between the office and home, as well as the workweek and weekend, is less clear. Technology can mean that you're always "accessible" via email, phone, text or chat. This means that, even if you commonly work from the office, you might also work from home too—on evenings and weekends. As you learn more about the team, seek to understand their definition of "accessible" and how it differs from "available." In those non-working hours, are you expected to respond within a certain timeframe (or is there a precedent or preference in place on the team) or can you respond if you choose to and leave until the next work day if you have other plans?

There might be a time in your life where you are willing to have a job that requires a significant time commitment. Perhaps you're particularly passionate about the work you're doing or there are meaningful financial rewards tied to your contributions. Those factors may make the extra work worth it. In many cases, those incentives are not present, and if you want more boundaries or the chance to live your life outside of work too, you'll have to ask for clarity about how committed and connected the team or company will expect you to be (including when and how you take time off) from those you meet in interviews. Knowing whether or not you're in one of those phases of life where you can over-contribute to work relative to the number of hours in a day and whether or not this job might require it will be important to clarify. You'll also need to assess how the team establishes and maintains boundaries between work and life so that you understand what space you'll have to do the things you want to do to rest, recover, and re-energize.

2.7 *Career Path*

Some people know early on what they hope their long-term career path will look like, or even the culminating role or accomplishment they aim to achieve. Others will find their path as they go or even explore multiple different paths while searching for the work that inspires, fulfills, or compensates them. There are many ways to move through your career. Some individuals might be focused on ascending through a particular promotion track, others might take lateral moves through different functions or departments, and some might find the role that will carry them throughout their career and stick with it. Whether you are looking to climb that career mountain, happy at the plateau, or seeking to find a role to build a home around, figuring out if your expectations are likely to be met by a particular role is beneficial.

Here are some questions to consider that might lead you to prioritize the career path available in your next role:

- Are you intentionally looking for career advancement?
- Is now the right time for you to focus on work?
- Does the role you take next need to confer value or signal specific skills or achievements to others?
- Is there a clear direction within your chosen discipline that requires or allows for a particular progression and/or timeline?
- Are you confident in the industry and/or company—that it has staying power, relevancy and prominence now, and over the next ten years?

- Is this the function you want to focus on long-term—will this role and the skills you develop serve as stepping stones to ongoing career opportunities?
- Is the ability to advance through roles in this company connected to career milestones you have identified and are working toward?
- Is having opportunities to learn and grow in your next role important to you?

Questions about career path or promotion opportunities come up frequently with candidates during the interview process. It makes sense in many regards. Candidates want to find out about future roles, growth, and rewards, as well as if the roles will provide the title, prestige, and learning they want in their career. To be able to effectively understand the potential career path at a particular organization, you'll need to evaluate it from various angles.

The average tenure at companies has decreased relative to prior generations. It also takes time, often multiple years, to develop the skills and operational familiarity that will result in a promotion. With that frame of reference, there's a good chance you won't be at the company to take them up on their career path progressions. Instead, you'll probably take new positions elsewhere to optimize your trajectory and total rewards. And, you'll make those moves on your own timeline, for the reasons and opportunities that matter most to you.

In reality, there may not be enough information for an interviewer to talk about career paths during the hiring process. Unless you're stepping into a role on a team where there is history and evidence of growth, advancement and acceleration for others, they may not have a clear perspective on what's next for someone like you. If you're joining a large team, where many people fulfill the same position and have for years, there is a better chance your interviewers can more accurately tell you what the potential pathways look like as well as what factors contribute to making those moves possible. If you are the first person to have this role, one of a small cohort, or if you are stepping into a new team, an interviewer can give you an answer, but you won't be able to know if it'll be true. If there is not an established process in place, are they giving you credible information or generic indicators to move the conversation along? It's hard to tell.

Additionally, it is unclear if your potential will equate to high performance. During the interview process, the company is assessing if they believe you have the potential to succeed. Can you effectively fulfill the responsibilities? Do you have the capabilities and skills? Will you approach the work with engagement, passion, and performance that differentiates you relative to peers?

And finally, it is also uncertain if you will like "it" (the job, the team, the city, the work, etc.) enough or care long enough to perform, stay, and succeed in progressive roles to get that desired promotion, or if you'll even want it when it's offered. The grass is always greener…

There are fields in which a clear career trajectory still exists, but there are many more where the thing to focus on in a new role is whether the skills you learn are applicable to a wide number of future opportunities. Careers, jobs, companies, and industries are changing fast, and one of the best things you can do for your career "path" is to treat it flexibly. The most important factor in having a long-term career path is deciding that the job you are interviewing for is the job you want and then succeeding throughout the interview process so that you get the job. This book is one of the tools that will help ensure you pursue and have access to the career path, whatever that might be, that best suits your aspirations and goals.

2.8 *Company Mission*

Why a company exists, the problems the team is focused on solving, and the steps they'll take to get there represent aspects of the company's mission and goals. A company's mission is its reason for existing. Some companies treat their mission statements like inspirational quotes about changing lives, or the world. Others are more straightforward: to provide a product or service that people need. The work that the team does, as well as the goals the business is focused on, is tied to that purpose, that reason for being. The mission, and the underlying goals and values that the company has will drive decision making, influence team structure and role design, and help shape the culture. In mission-driven organizations, the pull to participate and make a difference is a leading factor why people choose to work there and the resulting camaraderie and commitment can create a unique environment.

To determine whether or not a company's mission and goals will rise to the top of your priority list, consider the following:

- Are you purpose-driven when it comes to your career?
- Is there a cause that you want to commit to working on professionally?
- Do you need to believe in the underlying "why" to commit to a company?
- Is it important for you to be able to connect your work to higher-level company initiatives and outcomes?
- Does the company's mission resonate with you?

Most companies will highlight information about their mission on their website. Finding the "About Us" or "Mission" sections will help you gather information. Spend some time reviewing this content. A connection to the mission, or the absence of one, can have a significant impact on your experience. If you are passionate about a cause, being around people who are working toward related goals can be energizing. On the other hand, if you are not deeply committed to the work or end outcome, it can be isolating, even demoralizing.

Throughout the course of the interviews, listen for clues about how the mission influences the experience and work. Consider how often the topic comes up in interviews and how the team members talk about what it means. Are the signals that you hear and see in line with your level of attachment and interest in supporting the end goal of the company? Would you feel comfortable if you were a contrarian or apathetic participant in company meetings or initiatives?

◇ IMPORTANT   It's also important to learn how the team works toward the company mission as well. If you are excited about their "why," but disagree with how the company is tackling the problems and opportunities or have concerns about who they are partnering with to achieve results, the mismatch could be disheartening or troublesome. It's worthwhile to determine who "wins," when the company succeeds (investors, executives, employees or customers). Are those who have the potential to benefit the most the people you'd be excited to support and cheer on along the way?

2.9 *Company Goals*

Once you understand and assess the company's mission, it's time to understand how the organization's goals are structured. Some companies can plan effectively multiple years out and cascade relevant information, goals, and responsibilities throughout the organization. When you're interviewing with a company with that level of sophistication into their multi-year planning, you'll be able to ask about their objectives and get reliable information in return. Many companies, especially early-stage startups, are still working on next week or tomorrow and the ability to pinpoint specific initiatives or outcomes multiple months or years out is... out of the question. There may be ideas or aspirations, visions, and dreams, you should explore with your interviewers, but you can't put too much weight into information that falls into one of those categories.

The sophistication of a company's goal-setting process, communications, and ability to cascade and distribute that information effectively throughout the organization will vary significantly. A scrappy, small company might do this well with a refined approach, accurate data, and synchronized responsibilities and cross-functional efforts. Some of the world's top companies might be successful despite a broken or overly complicated and slow goal-setting process that is disconnected from most employees' experience. It's valuable, if not imperative, to care about the purpose the team is working toward and understand the categories of goals they will focus on in the near term (often tied to revenue, growth, margin, client, or customer satisfaction). The "what," "how," "how fast" and "with whom" are the type of details that you'll have to push to learn more about during the interview process.

With that in mind, prioritize getting a very clear picture of what's going on right now concerning how the team operates and what they view as their organizational strengths or weaknesses during the interviews. The more you know now, if "now" sounds exciting and aligned with your aspirations, the better you can feel about "later." If you can get behind the current initiatives and see yourself working well with the people who are on the team and find yourself curious about how a particular project might turn out, those are good signals. Perhaps that company is a place where, regardless of where they or you end up in 5–10 years, you'll have benefited from the experience.

When it comes down to the position specifically, the professional goals you'll be working toward and measured against are likely to be fluid, dynamic, and subject to evolving conditions. Hiring managers know the pain they are currently experiencing and the desired immediate solutions. If it's an established company they might also have a general idea of the rhythm of work, how it plays out throughout the year and over time. If that's the case, then they can probably share a realistic goal, but the problem there is that they could be resistant to change. The work may trend toward evolution rather than revolution—you might not be part of building something new, innovative, or challenging to the status quo.

Conversely, if it's a new position at a startup or rapidly changing company, there is a good chance they haven't thought that far out—they don't have time. They are solving to survive and it's better to understand if you're excited by the current problems, pain points, and people, and open to the unknown, uncertain shifts that are likely to occur. Are you comfortable with ambiguity, changes, and risk or do you prefer stability and certainty? If the value proposition changes, how will you respond? If the role is on the dynamic, uncertain end of the spectrum, the good news is that you might have the chance to influence the path forward. By the time you get oriented to the existing expectations and make progress toward the known goals, you'll have insight about what else needs to be done and how your background and expertise could contribute to the long-term impact. For this to be true, you have to find out how open your future manager and organization are to individuals driving the process.

And if we haven't all figured this out yet, the world can throw curveballs into any company's plans. Long-standing companies can fail, previously unknown products can quickly change our lives, and economic, political, or other global influences can impact how companies adapt and respond. It's impossible to pick the winners, but you can pick your team.

2.10   *Company Operations*

As you search for opportunities and pick roles to pursue, another important factor to consider is where a particular company is on their journey as well as how that stage impacts the way the organization operates. The way work gets done, and the philosophy and technology that drive a company's operations, can impact not only your day-to-day, but your overall experience and success.

In order to determine if a company's operations supports your ability to do your best work and if that is something you want to focus on in your job search, think about these questions:

- Is the company a brand new startup or established player?
- How comfortable are you with change and ambiguity?
- Is the company launching the minimum viable product, a new product or iterating and improving upon existing products?
- What does the organizational hierarchy look like and will it impact decision making, approvals, or access to information?

The way a company operates will influence how work, collaboration, communication, and outcomes are experienced and achieved. I've found that the size, revenue, or maturity of a company are not always the best indicators of where they are on their journey. I have another way of thinking about it, which is easier to get at during interviews. When calibrating across different opportunities, the metric I find most helpful is about "process."

- **Teams (or companies) with no process.** There are teams and companies at all stages with no process in place for good, dubious, or concerning reasons. As you interview, you will get hints about lacking or absent processes associated with the work you would do. Stepping into a role where this is the case will require hustle, creativity, research, and problem solving, and a lot of hard work. These opportunities are great for those with a builder's mindset, who aren't flustered by ambiguity and who can be resilient through changes over and over (and over) again.
- **Teams with emerging processes.** These are teams where they have initial and functioning processes mapped out and operational. The primary challenge is about scale or efficiency. Stepping into a role where this is the case will require systems thinking, the ability to connect the dots, and a commitment to collaboration and compromise. These opportunities are great for those who thrive on enabling human processes with technology, and who get excited by transforming spotty or chaotic processes into highly reliable, high performing ones.

- **Teams with established processes.** These are teams where they have working, scaled, and distributed processes in place. Stepping into a role where this is the case will require a precision mindset and a commitment to optimizing and refining on the margins. These opportunities are great for those who like to be part of broader initiatives and play a more defined role, and who prefer a more steady cadence to the rhythm of work.

- **Teams with outdated and cumbersome processes.** These are teams where the processes have been in place for so long and are so embedded in the way the company operates and delivered that they are both critical to success and a primary source of complaints. Stepping into a role where this is the case will require a patient mindset and the ability to mobilize across teams, leverage distributed resources and move forward in incremental and often slow steps. These opportunities are great for those who can see the chance to innovate in anything, and who are comfortable with longer-term time horizons to see change along with a more consistent state for their role and responsibilities.

> 🔊 STORY I've had the chance to operate on teams and in companies with processes at each of the stages outlined above, and there are positive aspects and challenges to each situation. At this point in my career, I'm more of a "no process" or "emerging process" kind of person, but someday that could change, and it wasn't always the case. I realize that my time spent with "established" and "outdated and cumbersome" processes has also been beneficial. It accelerated my ability to build, adapt, and transform in environments with "no" or "emerging" processes because I had models to work from and incorporate into my work. In anticipation of interviews, start to think about where you prefer to be in the journey of a particular team or company. Then during the interviews, ask questions of the hiring manager,[§4.2] direct reports,[§4.10] and cross-functional colleagues[§4.8] about the process to gain more context about how your preferences would align with their circumstances.

2.11 *Company Reputation*

Choosing a new role and working at a specific company has implications now, and later. There are certain companies that inspire trust, others that are recognized for their innovation, social impact, or growth, and some that are known for developing exceptional leaders across a number of disciplines. On the other hand, some companies rise and fall, are known for toxic leaders and internal strife, terrible customer experiences, or failed products, and are the subject of editorials and exposés. Some companies that have amassed billions in funding or revenue can be the same companies with bad reputations in other arenas.

The surprising reality is that companies on either end of the spectrum can offer valuable learning, growth, and opportunities, so it's up to you to decide how the company's reputation on different fronts will impact your decision. As you reflect, consider:

- Do you need this role/company to be a launchpad for future opportunities?
- What aspects of a company's reputation matter to you?
- How have previous experiences shaped your ability to respond to issues or take part in change and transformation?

In order to determine if this stop on your career journey will be worthwhile, think about the "dirt" you might discover and how significant it will be to you and your success.

If you're wondering, "dirt" is what everyone on the outside loves to talk about and what those on the inside hope to hide, especially during the interview process. It's the information you find when you go looking—employee reviews, rankings on top employer lists, podcasts, press releases, and product placements. Sometimes it's as simple as broken tools, outdated technology, or cumbersome processes; other times it's more complicated—toxic personalities, manipulation, lack of strategy, too much or too little on the roadmap, a vision without substance, systemic racism, harassment, or unclear and unachievable goals. The "what" may be unique to each company, but there is dirt, somewhere, everywhere, under... there. It's important to know what that dirt is before you make a decision. Because the existence of dirt is universal when it comes to companies, it's mostly about awareness and a conscious decision to choose the dirt in one place over the dirt in another. The dirt you know vs. the dirt you'll come to find hiding in places you hadn't had access to or anticipated during the hiring process.

You will need to get under the surface. The canned answers that someone shares as part of the standard interview process might be far from the truth. As an experienced interviewer and hiring manager, I had polished, positive answers reframing anything "tough" ready to go, including answers to the questions about my own failures and choices. Every now and then, someone would ask me a question that would make me pause, look up, and then back at them and say what actually came to my mind, abandoning the words I'd carefully prepared in case that line of questioning came up.

If you begin to ask tough questions and get to the end of an interview process without insight into the dirt, it's a chance to reflect. No dirt? Nothing wrong? Not possible! Try to ask another question or come at it from a different angle. On the other hand, if someone offers flags or if there is an issue or concern that emerges out of every conversation, a hint of something that just isn't right, listen, push, and probe. Don't worry, this can be tough, which is why I've prepared a list of questions in the Ask Me This Instead section§5 to help you get the information you need. The proactive slips, misses, and gaffes are very telling. Sometimes it's sabotage, other times it's evidence that, even in a context where people are supposed to be polite, diplomatic, and restrained salespeople, there is enough of something going wrong that they just can't hide it.

Once you know the dirt, weigh the magnitude of the flags and flaws you discovered. Chances are, they will seem worse and more complicated than they are to those inside. Are they the problems you might enjoy solving? Are you OK with conflict, complexity, or chaos? There are good problems for every type of person. The problems I love to solve would make someone else run away! It's about finding and balancing the problems and potential that are best for you.

2.12 *Employee Reviews*

Before interviews, one of your primary sources for learning about employees' experiences working at a particular company is the internet. There are endless websites with content and information including The Muse[13]

---

13. https://www.themuse.com/

and city-focused Built In[14] sites as well as sources for employee reviews and rankings such as Glassdoor, which can provide interesting tidbits and candid feedback. As you read through the information, try to balance it with your own real-life experience as you go through interviews as many of the inputs are anonymous and thus hard to qualify. What didn't work for someone else, could work well for you—no two employees will have the same experience even given similar circumstances or timing at a company.

Beyond the sites we might seek out when we're doing research, we're inundated by messages about work everywhere we go. While scrolling through your LinkedIn feed you see updates from your network about the exciting jobs someone's just started or the company milestones that they're "so lucky" to be around for. Sometimes, you'll see an intriguing headline about great perks or high salaries and click into it. It's hard to escape. Those messages, particularly the constant flow of them, can be helpful or disruptive at different periods during our career. Those messages can also be very persuasive. When targeted by messages with positive "filters," we're likely to fall prey. Especially on those hard days, the days when we're down or disappointed. The days when our boss or coworkers frustrate and exasperate us. The days when someone else gives notice, and excitedly talks about their new opportunity and we wonder, "What do they know that I don't?" Spoiler alert—they don't necessarily know anything more than you do.

◇ IMPORTANT It's important to read reviews and social posts with a thoughtful and objective perspective. Think about when people write reviews or share content to their social feeds. Actually, no, don't think about people, think about yourself. When have you been moved to share your thoughts or opinions with people who you don't know and likely won't meet? My experience has led me to think of three primary situations when people post work-related content:

1. When they were bragging, inspired, or excited—these are the new jobs, company milestones, and heartfelt messages.
2. When they were raging, ruminating, or shocked—these moments are prime fodder for anonymous review sites.

---

14. https://builtin.com/

3. When they've been asked or incentivized to do so—perhaps to push a big announcement or balance out something negative.

It's those polarizing experiences that compel us to seek reactions, validation, and camaraderie or commiseration. Read reviews and social posts with those frames in mind and with the recognition that you don't know the context behind the narrative they are sharing. These precautions do not invalidate the experiences or feelings shared by the person behind the screen, but help remind you that these are but one input in a long list that can be used to shape your thoughts about a particular role or company.

If during the interview process you want to ask about something you read on these sites or in an article, do it! Especially about those tough reviews—give an interviewer who you think is in a position to respond to the feedback the chance to provide their own or the company's point of view. You might appreciate their insight and you'll certainly learn something about how they respond to challenges and feedback as part of the broader experience and reputation associated with the company.

One final note, a significant portion of the content you'll find on sites is paid for and promoted. It doesn't mean it's untrue, but it is placed, polished, and a bit of theater, which means that there is a layer of authenticity missing. Perhaps the company is building its employment brand and took advantage of a content pitch for a piece that's part of a package, or it might be a promotion to pair with a strategic launch or announcement. It could also be damage control. In general, it's contrived and strategic messaging and you can consider it an advertisement of sorts. Take it, along with all information you receive, and use your critical reading, processing, and personal experience to assess the truth.

2.13 *Employee Experience*

One of my least favorite questions to be asked by candidates during the interview process was some version of, "What's the culture like at [COM-PANY]?" Because I was asked this question so often, I had many handy responses to rotate through or customize to the candidate I was speaking with, but those answers were never really that great. Culture, for me, is a living, breathing experience made up of and dependent on the behaviors, words, and actions of individuals, team, and the company collectively.

There can be dominant themes, and also micro-patterns, present in different pockets of the organization.

And what matters most about culture is a special combination for each and every person. I knew my answers about culture didn't stack up to reality, but with such a generic question, I often couldn't do much more. Eventually, I started asking a follow-up question of the candidate to ask them to specify a particular aspect of the culture that they wanted me to talk about so that I could give them information that they might actually find useful rather than a pre-packaged blurb that could have been copied/pasted at one of many different companies.

Because culture is so hard to grasp, I now focus on and emphasize the "employee experience" working somewhere rather than the culture. You can get at "an experience" in much more tangible ways through questions, conversations, and observations throughout the hiring process. They are the foundation of what you might choose to label as culture, and since that's what I know hundreds of people have asked me about, they are the topics I want you to diligently investigate at each step of the hiring process.

When it comes to employee experience, consider the following:

- How does the company present itself on the careers page? Are there video games or volunteer days? Pictures of a beautiful office or an overview of benefits? Does the company's "personality" come through?
- Do you get a glimpse of the makeup of the team? Is it inclusive or homogeneous?
- Do you see evidence that people bring their full selves to work? For example, personal photos on their desks, Pride or Black History Month posters, or a dress code that lets people freely show their personality and style?

The actual office or work environment often gets bundled into the employee experience or marketed as a key element of the value proposition. It makes sense, the office is easy to photograph and is something that is generally consistent for the onsite team. If you're interviewing for a role where you'd be in an office, take in what you see and consider how the environment will work for you. For example, if you know an open workspace is a distracting and unproductive environment for you and that is how their space is set up, ask about the availability of private or quiet workspaces for when you need to focus or if you have the ability to work from home to get a key project complete.

For individuals who have accessibility or health needs for a specific type of space or workstation, ask those questions to the person who is most likely to be informed or able to share accurate information and partner internally to get to the desired outcome. In some cases, you will be able to see their commitment—do they include accessibility information in their interview materials; are there all-gender restrooms available; is there a functional and comfortable lactation room; do the desks and office chairs adjust to different sizes or ergonomic needs, etc.? These questions are best directed to someone in HR who can work through a dialogue about reasonable accommodations for a specific position or worksite while maintaining the appropriate level of privacy and confidentiality. Though it can be difficult to raise these questions during the interview process, understanding whether or not the company not only fulfills the legal obligations but meets your needs is important.

Although many companies and teams were already working remotely in some capacity, the pandemic of 2020 ushered in a new point of view for many on the importance of remote and flexible work arrangements for roles where it is possible to do the work from home and on distributed teams. In the past, some companies prioritized the in-office experience for a variety of reasons including collaboration, community building, perceived productivity, and tradition. With the sudden and extended requirement to work remotely, teams adapted in ways they hadn't previously thought possible, incorporating new tools and tactics to get the work done, collaborate under a new context, and continue to move the business forward.

If the role you are interviewing for is going to be remote, understanding how the team approaches distributed work, whether or not they have been doing this successfully for a long or short period of time, the tools and technologies the team uses and how they cultivate community and collaboration at a distance is important. As for the "office," which may now be in your bedroom or kitchen, ask§5 about the budget or equipment provided to set up your workspace.

The pandemic experience will transform the way many companies approach their office space and the way they expect their team members to show up, but even out of that context, confirming that the way the team operates and how it's evolved will help you make sure it's an environment that works for you.

2.14 *Activity: Rank Your Top Priorities*

Thinking about your priorities is only the first step. To pursue them requires an extra layer of attention and intention. Putting your priorities at the foundation of your job search enables and empowers you to focus your efforts and target the roles and companies where you're most likely to find your match.

If you do not put yourself at the center of the search, the company's priorities will take precedence throughout your conversations and in the final outcome.

Use this section to proactively articulate what you're prioritizing at this stage in your career. Once you write it out, you'll find yourself evaluating everything—a job post, a benefits package, a prospective team dynamic—more confidently.

> Find the activity in this Google Doc![15]

2.15 *A Job Title Is Just a Starting Point*

◇ IMPORTANT Titles matter so much and also not at all. During the job search, titles help you align your understanding of how your experience, career stage, and existing leveling might transition into an open role. Similarly, the titles on your resume will help others understand how they might work with you. Some companies will use industry or functional standards for their titles and others will have bespoke titles because the job doesn't exist somewhere else. Companies may also label the same or similar work in distinct, unique, or seemingly contrary ways, even within their organization! A director at a Fortune 100 is quite senior within the organization and often deep into their career, whereas a director at a startup might run a function and have seniority within the company early on. Their experience and expertise is unlikely to be the same, though the value that each brings to their organization can be significant.

15. https://www.holloway.com/amti-worksheet

Occasionally during the recruiting process a title evolves or changes because the team learns more about what they are actually looking for and makes a more precise commitment to a level or framing. Perhaps the original title wasn't attracting the right talent or the right talent changed the context for the role, and subsequently the best way to label it. In other scenarios, the team is testing titles—putting out the same or similar job descriptions under separate titles to see what attracts the people they're looking to hire.

The variability, the evolution, the testing are all possible scenarios. What's most important is for you to understand what the label represents and determine if it matches your expectations and aspirations. If the title doesn't, but everything else lines up, it might be worth doing some research on how comparable organizations title similar roles in order to start a dialogue with the hiring team about whether a change is possible (note, I'd only do this at the late to final stages—it could be too disruptive to the process early on).

How should you think about titles? Titles are chapter labels in the career story but not indicative of the identity or value of the person who has them. After all, we don't normally get to pick our titles, someone else does or some structure sets them for us. Titles are signals, but we still have to help others cut through the noise. Find ways to understand the "what," "how" and "to what impact" when you're learning more about a particular role and calibrate your experience to their frame of reference. Through it all, don't let titles, your own or those on the job description, limit you. As you do your research and preparation, expanding your search criteria and focusing on what is highlighted within the responsibilities and qualifications section will open up new roles that may be a match for what you're looking for. Your current title, or the one at the top of the posting, should not be limiting factors into the positions you consider applying to. Working with the right people, on the right problems, toward a meaningful purpose at an appropriate pay rate will mean more now, and over time, than a word or two on your resume or LinkedIn profile.

2.16 *Activity: Assess the Landscape*

In order to find the right opportunities to pursue, you need to expand your search and become aware of the broader landscape of opportunities that could be available to you. This exercise will bring you from the starting point of a single title to a more comprehensive view of the type of roles that encompass the type of skills and abilities you possess (with any number of different titles!).

By opening up your search, you will generate new leads, ideas and possibilities for your career. More awareness about what exists as well as a habit of research and preparation will help ensure that when you discover a role you're very excited about, you'll be able to move forward deliberately and with confidence.

> Find the activity in this Google Doc![16]

2.17 *Activity: Create a Personal CRM*

Don't just search for jobs, look for people and keep track of them!

> Find the activity in this Google Doc![17]

2.18 *Break Down a Job Description*

The truth behind most job descriptions is that they are lightly edited, kind of plagiarized, branded marketing documents with a lot of words that often don't say that much. Once hiring managers know they have an opening, they think of the most common label that exists that represents the position they have in mind and put it into a search engine. This results in a bunch of job descriptions from other companies. With all these examples, they begin to skim them and pull out the "best parts," copying them into a document before massaging them into a more coherent and relevant version to post (or simply doing a "find and replace" for the other company and substituting their own). Oh, and they try to make it sound fun and compelling (you'll learn, you'll make a difference, we're changing

---

16. https://www.holloway.com/amti-worksheet
17. https://www.holloway.com/amti-worksheet

the world, and free beer on Fridays!). They do their best to make this job, this work, this grind, sound appealing or at least more appealing than the grind that you know or that other companies might be offering.

It's almost impossible to encapsulate the experience of a job in a short list of bullets, even if you start from scratch. Because of that, most job descriptions are also too long—both in the list of responsibilities you'll have and the qualifications you're supposed to bring. And yet, when we're searching for a job we tend to believe them. It's magical thinking. One way to ground yourself in this reality is to stop everything you are doing right now and look at your company's careers page. Do the job descriptions sound like they represent the work and environment that you experience every day?

Although job descriptions might try to make it seem otherwise, there are few truly original jobs. You might have had this realization while searching and comparing titles. Because the job description as a "tool" is so broken, you have to look beyond, dig deeper, and discover what is actually going on for this position and within this company. To do this, you need to break down a couple job descriptions.

2.19 *Activity: Break Down a Job Description*

Once you have found several postings that you're drawn to, pick two to break down. This will help on multiple fronts. First, it'll help you more quickly and critically evaluate job descriptions. It will also help you tailor your application materials and will kickstart your reflection on your experience in anticipation of interviews. Remember, you may not be able to check off every line of the job description, and that's OK!

> Find the activity in this Google Doc![18]

3 Write a Resume That Tells Your Career Story

Once you think you've found the job you want, it's time to move to the next step—preparing to apply and interview. Yes, preparing. If you have really found the job you want, don't send off a resume on an impulse! Time is of the essence, but sending off an incomplete or rushed resume or application could shut the door now, and for future opportunities. Once you have your target roles and companies, it's time to build your collateral. For now, a resume and LinkedIn profile are still part of that solution. The flaws of the job description are mirrored by those we all put into our own marketing documents—our resumes. Truthfully, the resume is a relic that definitely needs to be innovated. We spend countless hours writing bullets that make sense to us but that might not connect with anyone else. We curate a document that highlights what we think are our top or most impressive accomplishments, but that might not reflect our real capabilities or our interests. We edit the statements over and over for space, change the vocabulary so much so that often what we end up with is a list of generic jargon.

◇ IMPORTANT Just because the resume structure is outdated doesn't mean your experience isn't compelling, or that your passions and what you want to learn aren't important when seeking a new opportunity. My approach to building out your resume will help you see your experience holistically to bring out the best of what you've accomplished. It'll take extra work—more than dusting off the last version and adding some new bul-

---

18. https://www.holloway.com/amti-worksheet

lets. In fact, you're going to start thinking about your resume as a story. Perhaps you haven't thought about your resume as a story before. But if you take a storytelling approach to reflecting on your experience before you craft a document, you will unlock a more interesting and comprehensive version of your experience. As an added benefit, thinking through the events, people, and context is valuable interview prep as it enables you to add more nuance and depth to your responses.

To start, you're going to begin to view yourself as the central character on a journey with heroes and villains, struggles and successes, learnings and legacies. This exercise will help make this process less of a task... you might actually enjoy it (maybe just a little bit).

I urge you not to skip this exercise! Remember that resumes get only a few seconds of attention at key decision points in the hiring process. The reader skims the highlights—employers, titles, progression—and quickly determines if the remaining bullets are worth reading. Relevant, compelling, well-written bullets keep the reader focused and engaged. Unfortunately most resumes are full of the same kind of meaningless jargon and exaggerations as a typical job description and show very little of the person behind them. Remember, you're not just trying to get any job, you want to get the *right* job, and you can only do that by showing up as who you really are. This activity will help your resume stand out from the pack, keep the attention of your reader, and increase the likelihood of your getting an interview with a company you'll actually want to work at. It will require a mindset shift to share your experience in a new way. It'll be worth it.

3.1 *Identify Your Main Characters*

- **The Protagonist.** You! This story is about what you want and need—a new job. Your resume needs to include the information that puts you on the best path to get to your end destination. Think through the moments you're most proud of, the feedback you've received, the contributions, and impact you've made in each of your roles, and what you've learned.
- **Other Primary Characters.** Along the way, you've worked with and met people who have influenced your story and success. Understanding their influence as well as thinking about the context of your rela-

tionships will unlock plot points you might not have previously considered adding to your resume. What type of characters should you think about?

- **The Heroes.** There are surely people who have inspired you, pulled you along and served as role models throughout your career. You may envy their abilities at the start, until you realize the hero will help you see your potential and achieve it. Whom have you admired, who shined the light on your capabilities and cleared the path for you?

- **The Villains.** Every now and then, you encounter someone who makes work harder, frustrates and exasperates you and seems to find joy in crushing your spirit, productivity, or results. There are important insights to be garnered from your experience with villains that may represent some huge lesson, impact, and growth in your career. We often tend to put these experiences aside, but I recommend you evaluate them closely to see what positive results came out of them (especially as there will be a lot of interview questions that you can connect back to these experiences!).

- **The Crew, Squad, or Posse.** When have you been better because you were together? Thinking about the people who were by your side during periods of peak performance or intense creative collaboration as well as the day-to-day will lead you to remember moments and challenges that you wouldn't recall if you were only thinking about yourself.

- **The Teacher.** Hopefully you've had a manager, mentor, or colleague who took you under their wing and accelerated your ability to be effective in a given role. Think about people from across the companies you worked with who opened your mind about new ways to solve problems or who pushed you to gain the skills you needed to progress and advance.

- **The Protégés.** As you have developed expertise and experience, who did you support along the way? How have you built stronger peers or direct reports by stepping in and stepping up to support collective outcomes? When did your insight or contribution change the way others approached a problem or project?

Like in any good story, characters may switch between roles as they learn, grow, and evolve... or devolve. I've had villains become valuable members of my crew and heroes fall to the dark side. Those can be particularly engaging stories to consider as you think about what interactions created the most growth or led to the most important professional relationships and experiences. You'll have the chance to workshop your resume at the end of this section[§3.6] and in the workbook.[19]

3.2 *Consider the Place and Time*

The setting, or place and time, are often included on a resume without much extra thought—this role was at that company, located in this city. Seems simple enough, right? In the most basic sense, that is the setting. However, now is the time to start to think about setting more broadly, specifically where the companies you worked at were in time and place, that influenced your experience. How you operate in a well-established company with hundreds of people is dramatically different than a high-growth startup. The distance the company traveled while you were there impacts your role and responsibilities and contextualizes why you might have pursued a specific path or hit certain roadblocks during your tenure. The more you can connect dots and make your experience come to life in relevant and specific ways, the more the hiring team will be able to assess if your skills and capabilities will be effective in their environment.

As you consider the setting, ask yourself about the situations below to reflect on how they might have evolved during your time in a particular position. This will surface new awareness about how you changed and grew in response to the world around you. With the context fresh in your mind, you might see the events and accomplishments through a new lens and with more clarity about the impact, reasoning behind, or significance of a particular experience.

---

19. https://www.holloway.com/amti-worksheet

EXAMPLES OF PLACE OR TIME	PROMPTS TO CONSIDER HOW THE SETTING IMPACTED YOU
Strong economy vs. recession	Were you able to choose the job you wanted, or did you have to take the job that was available? Did you have part-time or contract roles rather than a full-time, regular position? Did your trajectory (title or pay) flatten or slow down? Did you have to take a role outside your preferred industry or function? Did the company have layoffs or did your compensation and/or benefits decrease?
Location	Were you in a role at a company's headquarters or a smaller satellite? Were you in a city where there was a density of talent to hire and a strong team to work with and learn from? Were you in a larger city or market with diverse industries and opportunities that you could access or were there limits? How did a remote-first or distributed team structure impact your experience in previous roles?
Company success or failure	Were there periods of rapid growth (hiring) or contraction (layoffs, turnover) that impacted you? Did the company raise venture capital or go through a merger or acquisition? Did the company have a competitive advantage, was it disrupting an industry or fading out of relevancy? Were there news stories or features about the company, its leadership or products? Were these stories positive or negative? Was the company meeting or exceeding goals or missing expectations? Was there steady and consistent leadership or new executives stepping in and changing the course?
Your own place and time	Did you have a well-defined role or did you "wear many hats?"Were there training programs available or did you have to drive your own development? Were you just starting out in your career, hitting your stride, or angling for the next step? Was work a priority or were you more focused on other aspects of your life?

3.3 *Map Out Pivotal Moments*

Your career, like a plot, is made up of a series of events. There are events of a more significant magnitude—new jobs and promotions, for example. Then there are those that may seem small, but that are, upon reflection, deeply meaningful and important—perhaps that first tough conversation with a direct report or turning a bad relationship around.

Though time facilitates a natural sequence and order of the events that take place, it may not always be the most compelling way to tell your story, specifically within the context of a particular role or period of time. The moments that are most relevant, impactful, and indicative of the journey you've been on as the protagonist might need to be put into a structure that will catch attention, build suspense (OK, probably more like *interest* in this scenario) and keep the reader curious and wondering about what they will read next.

Start to think about events, accomplishments, and activities that were important to you at the various stages and steps of your career and that would be interesting to the reader (like a recruiter assessing your potential, a hiring manager wondering if you've got the capabilities, or a future direct report trying to see if you're someone they think they'll learn a lot from).

To refresh your memory about events that are important to your plot, ask yourself the questions below. These questions are not only helpful for crafting your resume, but also for practicing your answers to interviewers' questions.

- What were specific, high-impact initiatives that you contributed to?
- When did you take a bold or controversial stance?
- When did you achieve something unexpected under tight deadlines, or despite other obstacles and constraints?
- How did you change the outcome of a key decision or important project?
- When have you changed someone's perspective or challenged the status quo?
- When did you lack confidence, but persevere and achieve the desired outcome?
- If you were able to share your best work with a future colleague, what would you share?
- What would others consider your greatest success, and would you highlight the same thing?
- When has someone recognized you for an accomplishment, large or small?
- When did you adapt to surprises or change successfully?

As you take this new lens, you might change whether or not you include a specific accomplishment and how you combine and sequence as part of a larger whole. You'll start to see how the story comes together once you consider the relationship between the events, the characters who helped shape them, and the setting that influenced why things transpired the way they did. Your job is to thread all these points in time together so that they don't come across as random occurrences but a strategically threaded and cohesive progression of discovery, growth, and impact.

This will help them move through your resume and keep reading to understand not just what you can do but more about your progression and your potential. Who you are is more than what you've done!

3.4 *Include Tension and Conflict*

The desire to move beyond and even forget particular conflicts we have throughout our careers is natural. However, conflict in your career, like the tension in a story, is where some of the most interesting and important moments occur. In fact, these moments often represent the catalyst for characters to transform. Being able to articulate how these tests impacted you will add depth, interest, and a dose of reality to your resume. Without realizing it, you're also preparing for the interviews by thinking about the experiences that pushed you and those that you might want to avoid in the future. These memories can be helpful in building the list of questions you'll ask certain interviewers.

INTERPERSONAL CONFLICT	CONSIDER A BROADER LENS
Relationships that got off to a bad start that ultimately turned around	External factors that shifted timelines, product design, or even internal operations
The dynamics in meetings during periods of stress or high stakes	When a customer backed out of a deal or a colleague unexpectedly left the team
Trust, or rather the lack thereof, within a team or organization	Hard moments, unexpected changes, or big surprises
Failure that led you to quit, change course, fire someone	Times when you made a mistake or intentionally disrupted progress
The times you cried or lost your temper	A moment or experience that was embarrassing
Tough conversations	A period when you were bored or unengaged in your work
New hire or new manager changing the status quo	When you didn't believe in the company, its product, or people
Moments that made you look for another role	Lack of a feeling of belonging, being "othered," or needing to assimilate

As you reflect, acknowledge the frustration, pain, and problems, and the context that surrounded them. Then, think about what positive growth, lesson, or change happened as a result. That is where the magic lies and what will be most helpful as you craft your resume, prepare to respond to interview questions, and evaluate if you'd encounter similar challenges in a new role.

3.5 *Connect Your Story to Their Needs*

One of the reasons I recommend taking the storytelling approach to updating your resume is that it helps you think about your journey and accomplishments in a new light. When confronted with a blank document, the pressure to put the "right" examples down is real and there is a tendency to fall into self-doubt. This can result in bullets that are bland (when you're writing something to fill space) or even untruthful (when you don't think a particular bullet is strong enough so you modify the details to sound more impressive). Then, because many people write resumes in isolation without feedback from those who worked with them or know them well in a professional capacity, resumes often fail to capture the reader's attention—and that's the entire point! Recruiters and hiring teams want to connect dots quickly between candidates and their role. Think about what they are looking for and how you can specifically and clearly connect your experience to their needs.

◇ **IMPORTANT** If time and capacity were unlimited, resumes should be customized to a specific company and role. Because that level of tailoring often requires more time than you have available, consider developing one or two versions, each emphasizing a unique angle on a potential company's needs. For example, you might be open to manager and individual contributor roles. Consider framing one resume about management and leadership, going deep into your ability to get results through others via coaching, delegation and feedback. For the other version, you could focus on the depth of your expertise, technical or functional accomplishments, and examples of your ability to collaborate.

Or, let's say you are applying to a Fortune 500 company and a Series A startup. For the Fortune 500 company, you might choose to include more information about your cross-functional talents, project management capabilities, and communication skills. For the version you'd submit to the startup, you'd highlight examples of your flexibility and resilience, when you delivered results under pressure, and your ability to take on new and diverse challenges.

As you review job descriptions and begin to think about how your experience either directly or indirectly contributes to your ability to fulfill the different roles, remember it's rare for anyone to have a line for line match with a job description's "requirements"—do not let this deter you. For example:

- If the role you're pursuing has different goals than what your prior experience can speak to, take the chance to highlight the "how" more than the "what." Include details on the way you approached setting a goal and breaking down the milestones, along with indicators of how you tracked and measured success.
- If there is a new system or technology required that you don't have experience with, share details about similar technologies or your experience learning a new tool to get results.
- If the role is a management position and you've never led a team, incorporate information about your experience mentoring colleagues, leadership experience outside of work (in academic or volunteer contexts), or examples of when you made decisions or delegated work as a peer or project manager.
- If the role has an expanded scope over a workstream or team that you have not led before, reference your cross-functional collaboration, shared initiatives, or instances where you influenced the work product or outcomes for that function.

When you are connecting your experience with the responsibilities and requirements listed in job descriptions, make sure you expand your brainstorming. Your experience in academic programs or community organizations could demonstrate the skills needed. It's also a good time to reflect on feedback you've received. There, you might rediscover insights about learning and growth that are transferable. It is critical in these instances to give specific examples of curiosity, learning, impact or expertise that you believe is indicative of your ability to take on the responsibilities of this role. Simply saying you have a growth mindset or are a life-long learner is not enough! Take the opportunity to show the hiring team what you have to offer rather than just telling them.

3.6 *Activity: Translate Your Story Into a Compelling Resume*

> Find the activity in this Google Doc![20]

3.7 *Activity: Connect Your Story to the Roles You Want*

It's time to bring together all the previous activities, align your experience to key themes, and then select the most compelling examples of your experience to highlight under each role as you pull everything together into a resume.

> Find the activity in this Google Doc![21]

3.8 *Activity: Pair Your Resume with a Cover Letter*

Cover letters are one of the aspects of the application process that cause a lot of angst, confusion, and frustration. Candidates wonder if the hiring team even reads them or if the time they spent is wasted. While I cannot vouch for every company's application review process or every hiring manager's approach, when I'm recruiting I open the cover letters attached to applications as often as possible. I find they give new insight and add breadth and depth to the resume bullets, which are often generic. Though I cannot guarantee that everyone, or even someone, at the company will read your cover letter, refining your thinking and how you articulate your experience, readiness, and alignment with the requirements of the role is additional practice and preparation for you.

A well-written cover letter is a short, to-the-point pitch about why you are the candidate for this job. It should add something new about your experience and abilities to the application—building upon rather than restating what is in your resume. *If you cannot customize your resume to every position, you must tailor your cover letter!* To miss the chance to bridge your list of accomplishments and skills with their opportunity and highlight why you chose this position over others out there might mean you don't get to interview.

---

20. https://www.holloway.com/amti-worksheet
21. https://www.holloway.com/amti-worksheet

You don't have to overthink or spend hours crafting your cover letter. Building upon the framework below enables you to complement the information presented on your resume, customize the application to the company, and highlight some of what makes you a great candidate.

> Find the activity in this Google Doc![22]

3.8.1 COVER LETTER EXAMPLE

Dear A.R. Tatum,

As a customer of COMPANY, I know firsthand how effective the targeting and messaging of your marketing campaigns are and I want to join your team as the Director of Digital Marketing to play a role in your ongoing success.

From the earliest days of my career, I knew data-driven marketing was my passion. I followed my instincts through progressive roles starting with a stint as a Digital Marketing Specialist at a small startup where I focused on SEM and Analytics and then took on email, paid social, and display efforts. After several years, my former manager recruited me into a Digital Advertising Campaign Manager role at Amazon where I led a high-performing team responsible for >100 campaigns a month before being promoted to Senior Manager of Advertising Performance and Optimization.*

I build programs that get results across channels, whether starting from scratch or scaling and adapting existing efforts. As a leader, I partner cross-functionally to ensure our marketing strategy and metrics tie to business objectives and am a hands-on manager who believes that coaching and feedback empower individuals to succeed in their roles. I'm curious too—I follow industry leaders, research the latest tools and tactics, and continually analyze campaign performance to ensure we're testing, iterating, and executing the most effective campaigns possible.

---

22. https://www.holloway.com/amti-worksheet

I've spent years refining my expertise so that when my dream role came around, I'd be ready. The right role is COMPANY's Senior Director of Marketing. My resume highlights my accomplishments and quantitative examples that demonstrate how I can help COMPANY continue to drive customer acquisition and retention toward sustainable revenue growth. I look forward to exploring this opportunity with you soon.

YOUR NAME

4 People and Power in the Interview Process

The interview process is often just a few hours spread over several days or weeks. That is not a lot of time to get to know the company, responsibilities, and expectations, let alone all the people. You're going to spend 40+ hours a week over the course of many months or years working with these individuals. It's important to recognize each person's unique contribution to the process, work, and your experience. The people you spend your days with can transform the mundane into meaningful or turn a dream job into a toxic, miserable slog. Your interviewees are a small representation of the company in most cases (unless you're interviewing at a tiny company or new startup) and your time with them is your primary chance to get a window into the broader employee and team experience.

Throughout a standard interview process, you'll encounter a handful of prospective colleagues. Some of these interviewers could play a key role in your experience and others you will just know in passing, but they are all valuable guides to your future work experience. Each person brings a different lens to the company, role, and team and can unlock new perspectives and information that others wouldn't be able to share. Crafting a targeted set of questions for each interviewer profile that addresses specific areas of interest based on your established priorities will help ensure you efficiently and effectively gather information.

To get the best 360° view of the company, you'll need to take advantage of the opportunity to ask a tailored set of questions to each person. In this section, I'll explore the roles, personas and priorities of the people commonly involved in the interview process so that you can incorporate them into the plan you create later in this book. Some sections are more expansive than others—these are people who are more pivotal and influential in the recruiting process. For example, the recruiter is someone you'll almost always interact with, and the hiring manager is probably the most important person for you to get to know. In some cases, a single person can play more than one of the roles outlined, which is why it's so important for you to know who you are interviewing with, why, and what their role will be in the process. Remember that titles or roles do not always equate to influence or trust within the hiring team—anyone participating in the process could be the key vote or veto in interviews. Make sure you take an inclusive approach to engage with each one of your interviewers. Later, in the question section[§5] of the book, you'll see questions designed for each of these personas so that you can create your specific interview plan.

4.1 *Recruiter*

Put simply, the recruiter is your guide throughout the process. Often the first person you talk to, the recruiter wants you to succeed. This is both a positive and complicated reality as they have diverse motivations to consider throughout the process including, but not limited to, those of the hiring team, those of the candidate, and their own.

This is not a game of love, but there are parallels. Recruiters play the role of matchmaker. Recruiters spend time networking and interacting with lots of different people at any given time including hiring managers, candidates, external partners or agencies, cross-functional interviewers, and executives, and are constantly trying to understand, manage, and meet their varied expectations for the role, hiring process, and the eventual new hire.

They fulfill this responsibility with a combination of intuition, judgment, and influence. Even when someone (either an internal team member or a prospective employee) is being transparent and direct, there are "unsaid truths" that a recruiter has to reflect upon and process within the bigger picture. A talented recruiter is always listening, as they work to understand a broad set of factors to see where and how they will converge toward the desired outcome—getting the right person in the right role as quickly and efficiently as possible. Typically, recruiters are natural conversationalists and make that initial conversation relatively easy for candidates by conveying information, enthusiasm, and support.

Don't let the charm and openness distract you—recruiters are still responsible for assessing the alignment of your capabilities with an established set of criteria for the position, while also weighing your talent relative to other candidates and current employees to see who is the closest match on the most dimensions. There is nuance and subjectivity at play.

Many recruiters are expert assessors, with years of experience interviewing thousands of candidates. They know what great looks like and have a refined approach to asking the right questions and sharing relevant business or role context. Others are not experts. This may be because they are early in their recruiting career or unfamiliar with the real context of the role. They might run through a script, ask questions that have little to nothing to do with the role, and fail to listen to your answers.

While some recruiters specialize in roles of a specific nature, for example engineering and technical roles or sales positions, many internal recruiters are responsible for a wide variety of openings across functions, disciplines, and levels. In some companies, there may only be a single recruiter who has to support, source, and manage the hiring process for all openings. Because of the variability of the roles that most recruiters cover, it's important to remember that they are generalists, not specialists, in the domain of any particular position. This means they have a broad, not deep, understanding of the skills, day-to-day activities, tools, challenges, and context that someone who would step into the role would encounter or need to know.

Whether or not there is an internal team member working on recruiting, some companies also partner with external recruiters to support their hiring needs. External recruiters may be "retained" to fill a particular role, meaning they are paid up front and throughout the recruitment process to help the company find the right person. Or, they might be working on a "contingency" basis, which means they will only be paid a fee if they successfully find the candidate who accepts the job. The fees that external recruiters are paid are most often a percentage of the new hires' salary or projected total cash compensation (including bonuses, etc.). Because of these pay structures, these recruiters are eager to fill the position and, as a result, can be a proactive and supportive partner. It's important to note that, as external partners, they will likely have less insight and influence than internal team members and you will need to establish strong relationships with the people you meet in interviews to vet the information they provide and get the answers you need.

In an ideal world, all recruiters, whether internal or external, are a trusted guide and thoughtful facilitator for the duration of the process, providing insights on the next steps and requirements, communicating updates, and advocating both for candidates and the company. But sometimes, things won't play out like that. There are many reasons why not—and not all of them are within the recruiter's ability to control. Here are some of the scenarios that might be playing out behind the scenes that could influence your recruiter's ability to move the process forward or give you information:

- **The hiring team has competing priorities or poor communication.** Sometimes a recruiter can be on top of the process, actively engaging with and bringing viable candidates into the process, sharing feedback and recommendations with the hiring team, and getting crickets in response. They email, stop by, Slack, and text to no avail. In this case, the hiring manager may not be making recruiting a priority, may not be able to commit to a decision, or may have the answer but not the time or ability to pass that information along.
- **There may be changes to the process or role in motion.** Recruiting is a dynamic and evolving process. And it should be. If recruiters or hiring teams think they have the role and candidate profile precisely defined at the start, they are more likely to miss something important during the interview process. As conversations progress, the context changes too. The project or goals might shift, or team members might join or quit. Additionally, teams might learn something in early conversations with candidates that changes their perspectives on what matters most for the position.
- **A work and team environment is interconnected, and few decisions are really independent or discrete.** When something changes, there are likely downstream impacts that will take time to identify and resolve, which can delay a hiring process. In some cases, the recruiter will be aware of these evolving situations and able to provide updates. In other cases, they will be operating without an understanding of what's impacting the process or delays and might be just as frustrated as you are.
- **The hiring team may wait to move candidates forward pending the outcome of other interviews.** When you really want a job, it's natural to believe that you are the only candidate the team is considering.

In reality, they might have a handful of other contenders or a long list of applicants to sort through and manage at every step of the process. It's a helpful and even productive exercise to remind yourself of this along the way. It can help motivate you to continue to prepare and put your best self forward, and help soften the pain if you aren't the candidate selected. It's in candidates' and companies' best interest to make these big decisions with more than a single data point.

- **Because there are several candidates in the process, the team might want to accelerate or pause other conversations at certain points.** This is not necessarily a bad thing—if they have an offer out to someone else that they are excited about hiring, holding off asking you to come in for a full day of interviews saves you time and effort. It can be hard to balance the communication in these situations and some companies cannot or will not be transparent about why there is a pause. Be patient, proactive, and positive, checking back in to see if there are updates now and then. Just because this specific role might not work out doesn't mean there won't be other opportunities with this company at some point in the future. Though it can be frustrating, resist the temptation to be rude or impatient. If the process isn't well-run, consider it another valuable data point!

- **The business or economic context might change.** Hiring is impacted by other activities within a particular company as well as factors well beyond the business. For example, projects may be started or canceled, companies may make an acquisition or be acquired, startups might raise a new round of funding, new leaders might join a team and others might transition out, or the company might have an amazing quarter or completely miss expectations. These situations, and so many others, will determine if certain roles move forward in the hiring process or not. Of course, there is also the possibility that the world can change. A product or process might become outdated or unpopular, a new service or technology might disrupt an industry, or the economy might change due to local, national, or international circumstances ranging from government transitions to natural disasters to a pandemic. Smart companies will respond to these situations by prioritizing the roles that are core to the business' operations and long-term success. Their response requires tough decisions, sometimes eliminating new and open roles, rescinding offers and canceling programs, and sometimes laying off or furloughing existing employees. In either scenario, there isn't much you can do. Be gracious, positive, and responsive.

- **The recruiter might have too many "to-dos."** Perhaps you've been in a situation at work where you couldn't keep up with everything that was required and a few things fell through the cracks. Recruiters, who might be working on 7, 10, or even 40 roles at a given time, occasionally have things fall through the cracks too. For every one of those roles, there might be hundreds of applicants, dozens of conversations in progress at different stages, and endless back-and-forth with dozens of people and entities. It's important to ask questions[§5] to the recruiter about the target interview and hiring timeline, what next steps look like, and their typical approach to communication to give you the best chance of staging your follow-ups at the right time.

During the conversation, remember the recruiter is a gatekeeper to other conversations—their read on your qualifications and ability to do the work will play a role in whether or not you move forward in the process. Over-prepare for this conversation on all dimensions—learning about the company, team, and industry, thoughtfully reflecting on your experience, and practicing responses to potential interview questions. You might also want to get a pulse on new information you might bring into your conversation— read blogs, follow thought leaders, and pick a few nuggets that connect to your experience or fitness for this role, or demonstrate your knowledge of the field, dedicated interest, and curiosity. Finally, if you have questions about the "logistics," the recruiter is a good person to start with, though some questions are more suitable for later in the process, like about benefits or bonuses.

4.2 *Manager*

◇ IMPORTANT Put simply, a great manager can transform your career while you work with them and long after. Finding that kind of manager is magic and worth several percentage points on top of any salary. They influence so many aspects of your experience day-to-day and over time. As for the bad manager, think back on the vent sessions you've been a part of with team members, partners, and friends. What is one of the aspects of the work experience that everyone bemoans the most? Their boss. As a recruiter, I know this is one of the things candidates need to focus on the most throughout the hiring and decision-making process.

During the interview process, managers play the role of mentor, motivator, and evaluator. Their accomplishments and experience at work depend largely on the strength of their team. If anyone is more motivated than the candidate to find the right hire, it's the manager. In navigating the interviews, the manager must weigh the capabilities and experience of the candidate within their understanding of the work to be done as well as how this prospective hire will complement and extend the expertise and output of the rest of the team.

While they may seem to be all-knowing or all-powerful in the process, in most cases, the manager will not be. There will be other voices represented in the process, other interviewers for example, as well as other decision-makers, such as their boss or a more senior executive.

Many managers are natural leaders and develop their team members' skills and capabilities. They know what they're looking for, perhaps they even filled the role you're applying for themselves, and understand deeply what it takes to be successful in that role. These managers recognize potential and ability and can effectively bring out the best in a candidate and their direct reports. Other managers are new or developing in this capability, having recently made the transition from doer to leader, and might not be as effective or capable in structuring a collective body of work across a team of people, designing and scoping roles or interviewing to fill a gap. A lack of experience doesn't necessarily mean they won't succeed or be a great manager—it does, however, put an extra burden on you, as their prospective direct report, to understand their strengths and development opportunities, managerial and communication style and their expectations of whoever steps into the open role. On the flip side, an experienced or long-term manager might be ineffective or just bad at their job, too—years of experience doesn't always correlate to skill in the management capacity.

In an ideal world, a manager has had a role model to learn from or years of experience and success leading teams so that they approach the new position, hiring process, and onboarding of a new hire with attention and sophistication. If they are less experienced or skilled, a strong recruiting team and thorough process can fill in some of the gaps. But sometimes, they will be relatively alone in the process and might even be driving it from end-to-end with autonomy and limited oversight.

◇ IMPORTANT   It is of the utmost importance that you take advantage of every minute you have with your future manager, and if possible, ask for more time than they may have allotted during the process if you get to the final stages or receive an offer. As you progress through the course of multiple conversations with the hiring manager, continue to identify, map out, and ask thoughtful, tough questions.§5

Along with the real-time answers, take time after the interviews to do some extra reflection and diligence. Reflect on the chemistry and compatibility you sensed—or didn't—during the conversations. This is hard to quantify, and sometimes even harder to articulate. While I maintain that relying exclusively on your gut is a fallback that can be avoided by the kind of preparation I offer in this book, your instincts can still be a data point or factor. Your gut feeling can be very powerful and revealing as you determine if this is the person you need to be your manager at this point in your career. When I reflect back on the first conversation I had with two of my favorite bosses, I knew then—before we even got to interview questions—that they were managers I'd learn from and enjoy working with. I knew I'd become a better version of my professional self as a result of that relationship. Similarly, when I think back on the relationships that weren't as strong or beneficial straight out of the gate or as time progressed, there was something that just didn't click and I had to convince myself and rationalize away my hesitations to move forward. Unfortunately, the issues or lack of connection didn't go away. In fact, when the going got tough, the distance grew and the problems magnified, ultimately accelerating my decision to look for another role.

Finally, in an effort to check your gut, take the chance to verify that the manager is telling you the truth during the interviews. To do that, connect with others who currently and previously worked for them. As you go through the interview process, connect with interviewers on LinkedIn. Once you're connected, you can see where your network overlaps and potentially find someone who could endorse you or provide insight into the team and opportunity. These individuals will have different views, and it's important to understand that the context of the relationships and growth a manager experiences, as well as your unique interpersonal dynamics, will surely impact how your connection plays out with the manager. In the meantime, you can get a read on how they coach and develop, communicate and direct work, measure performance and share context, balance the struggles and celebrate success from these other conversations. After all, there's a good chance the company will check your references—why not look into theirs?[§4.11] I always thought that anyone who was considering working on my team should talk to the people who worked for me before—they would tell a much more accurate picture than the stories I'd craft about my style and approach. Find a way to get this insight by asking current or former direct reports targeted questions.[§5]

4.3 *Department Executive or the Boss' Boss*

Depending on the nature of the company, role, and makeup of the hiring team, you may or may not encounter the hiring manager's boss or a department executive. Even if you do not meet them, understanding their role and influence in the hiring process and your ultimate path at the company is valuable information to gather during interviews.

Put simply, this leader is responsible for the hiring manager's team's success and likely a broader scope of work. With this bird's eye view, they want to ensure there are capable, engaged, and talented individuals in each position and, importantly, that those individuals come together to form a high performing and productive unit working toward a collective set of priorities. The department executive is tasked with operationalizing a higher-level set of functional or company priorities and building an organization (vs. a team) that delivers. As with the hiring manager's motivations, a strong group of teams reporting to an executive enables and impacts their success so their attention and commitment to the process takes into consideration the full team's performance, capabilities, and expertise.

In most cases, the leader will have collaborated on, reviewed, or approved the job description. Depending on the size of the company or the seniority of the role, they may have weighed in on the content of the job description, as they help drive and delegate priorities and goals for the overall team. Typically more tenured in their career (though not always), a department executive will have institutional, industry, and team context that enables them to interview and evaluate with confidence and a perspective that is long-term and beyond the scope of many of the other interviewers. At the same time, they remain close enough to the details and day-to-day operations that they can credibly determine an individual candidate's strengths and gaps while calibrating and comparing those attributes across their teams.

In an ideal world, they participate in the process to assess, but more importantly to help paint a vision and clarify departmental and organizational goals and the related interdependencies and accountabilities. During your (likely limited) time with the department executive, try to capture their wisdom and insight on that next layer of context by asking thoughtful, targeted questions[§5] about the manager and team you'd work with. This is an important time to also prepare a clear, concise, and compelling elevator pitch about you—highlight your strengths, interests, and capabilities and directly connect them back to the position and the conversations you've had so far in the interview process. While this executive may not be an active participant in your eventual day-to-day, they will be a key voice and decision-maker in influential processes and milestones (like performance reviews and promotions decisions) as long as you're both on the team.

4.4 *Activity: Craft Your Interview Elevator Pitch*

The elevator pitch—what you say when you have 30 seconds to make an impression—is a great tool in the job seeker's toolkit. The elevator pitch can be used in passing at a networking event, or to kick off an interview with someone who may not be as close to the role or hiring process (like an executive). As you refine your job search to a specific type of role or company, having this quick pitch ready is in your best interest. (Having it ready means you've practiced actually giving it!)

> Find the activity in this Google Doc![23]

4.4.1 ELEVATOR PITCH EXAMPLE

> *My career started in marketing at a small startup and has progressed through roles as a Digital Advertising Campaign Manager and Senior Manager of Advertising Performance and Optimization at Amazon. I shine when I get to lead a team dri-*

---

23. https://www.holloway.com/amti-worksheet

ving digital advertising strategy and ad operations to efficiently improve campaign performance and deliver business results.

I'm curious about how I can apply my expertise within fintech, an industry I know is positioned for long-term growth. I've led high-performing teams in my career and am now focused on the chance to lead a department and help build a marketing strategy and organization from the ground up.

If I had the chance to step into the Director of Digital Marketing role, I'm confident my background and excitement about building data-driven, cross-channel marketing programs will enable me to support COMPANY in achieving customer and revenue growth.

As you went through this exercise, did it feel a bit like the cover letter? That's intentional. The cover letter and elevator pitch can complement and reinforce one another. In fact, reiterating the main points in more than one way is to your benefit. The elevator pitch is a supporting structure, not a script. The goal is to help you think through your experience so that you can practice a time or two (or ten!) on your own. Then, when you have the chance to share your pitch with someone, you won't have to recite a stilted script—you'll be confident enough to speak naturally and authentically without missing any of the key points.

4.5 *Activity: Craft a Thank-You Note*

If you want to get the most out of the effort you put into your elevator pitch, consider incorporating a very similar structure into your post-interview thank-you notes (or more likely, emails). It's not required to send a follow-up and it can even be controversial—after all, the company is looking for someone to fill their position, maybe they should send *you* a thank-you for coming in! But, if you view the follow-up note as a chance to highlight your candidacy, build a relationship with someone who could be a team member—now, or down the road—and to re-connect dots between your conversations and potential to contribute based on your post-interview reflection, taking a few minutes to send these notes can be worthwhile.

The most efficient way to do this is to add a personal sentence or two at the start of the elevator pitch structure highlighting why you enjoyed meeting a particular interviewer and an insight you took out of the conversation.

4.5.1 A THANK-YOU NOTE EXAMPLE

I really enjoyed our conversation yesterday. I have been thinking about the growth goals you mentioned and how I could bring experience building high-performing, scalable advertising programs to your organization. I thrive when I have the chance to immerse myself in the most important challenges the business is facing by building efficient operations to optimize performance.

With what I learned in the interviews, I can see clearly how I can apply my expertise within fintech and as the leader of this department. If I had the chance to step into the Director of Digital Marketing role, I'm confident my background and excitement about the opportunities and challenges the team is addressing would enable me to support COMPANY in achieving customer and revenue growth.

4.6 *CEO, Founder, or Other C-Level Exec*

Put simply, a chance to talk with someone in this position is incredibly valuable and they may play a variety of different roles during the hiring process. In smaller-stage companies or roles in their direct reporting lines, they may be evaluating you based on functional, industry or technical expertise, leadership potential, or a wide set of competencies and capabilities they believe are key to success in the particular role, and also within the overall organization. It's possible that they are close to the operations of a given team, project, or position, but don't expect them to spend time getting into the weeds and don't take them there with your questions (but do ask questions![§5]).

If you're interviewing at a large company or in an entry to mid-level role, you may not interview with the CEO. However, if you're pursuing a role at a small company or startup, there's a decent chance you'll be able to cross paths during the hiring process with the CEO, a member of the founding team, or another C-level executive. Regardless of the company size, C-level leaders and founding teams have to operate at the 50,000-foot view, bringing together diverse topics, priorities, people, and processes into a cohesive, structured, and viable path forward. In some ways, these senior leaders are accountable to "no one" (they don't have a boss), but they are also accountable to *everyone* (the full team, investors or board members, customers, shareholders and beyond).

In an ideal world, there is alignment from the leadership team all the way throughout and across the organization. In reality, that's tough, so focus less attention on the specifics of the position and listen to their insight on themes, long-term priorities, and aspirations for the team and company to get an impression of how their leadership flows throughout the organization. In anticipation of this conversation, refine your elevator pitch and do extra research on the company and the leader's background (by reading blog posts or articles, listening to podcasts, following them on social media, and watching interviews). During interviews, be prepared to speak not only to your own background and experience but a set of connected and expanded topics as well. This is a rare chance to demonstrate your presence, articulate your talents, and leave a lasting impression.

4.7 *Peer or Team Member*

There is a good chance you'll get to meet someone during the process who would be a peer on the specific team you'd join. This conversation can be a powerful glimpse into an important business relationship, and the information you'll gather from the interview as well as the questions that a peer might ask will illuminate critical elements of the role. Put simply, prospective peers are often closest to the details of the work to be done, understand the status, challenges and opportunities, and what it takes to be successful relative to the goals the team is responsible for achieving. They might also have a similar background or set of skills and capabilities and therefore ask very targeted or specific questions to evaluate your expertise and determine if you have the qualifications to meet the expectations of the role and work well with the team.

During the interview, they may play the role of a companion or partner that would be a trusted collaborator on projects and someone who will bring internal insight and context to support your integration and success. It's also possible that they will take a more competitive approach and step into the interviewer role as someone who is not necessarily a judge (they are not the hiring manager), but also not a friend. They may challenge you subtly or directly to test the boundaries of this potential relationship while weighing the trade-offs of how you might make their life better or potentially worse.

In an ideal world, people in these roles want nothing more than a super talented, smart, capable team member to work at their side, but others will be threatened if they believe you will outshine them, "take away" something they enjoy doing, or upset a status quo that works for them.

During your conversation with a peer, prepare to share your expertise thoughtfully and with an extra emphasis on humility and empathy. Hone in on the questions that they ask you—these are probably quite relevant to the problems you'd encounter and experiences you'd discover in the role. Listen for cues about the team dynamic and cross-functional collaboration that might be playing out at their level and therefore less visible to the management team. Ask as many questions as possible about the hiring manager and team and company leadership to suss out if the interviewer appreciates the direction, development, and support provided, and if they seem committed to the team and company. Look out for inconsistencies or flags that the leaders might be able to effectively avoid addressing or have a polished and convincing response prepped and ready to share.

You're going to spend a lot of time with your peers and strong relationships here can make the tough days easier, the wins more thrilling, and the journey from one role or stage to the next, one team or company to another, more fulfilling, and even more fun.

4.8 *Cross-Functional Colleague*

A strong company is rarely built in silos with a narrow group of functional experts driving the process or product development from end-to-end. With that in mind, most hiring managers will include relevant cross-functional team members in the hiring process. Cross-functional team members will be key contributors to company initiatives that are complex and large-scale, with dependencies rooted on the team and associated with responsibilities listed in the job description of the position you are targeting.

Put simply, both in the interviews and on the ground, cross-functional team members play the role of the translator—bringing their expertise and skills to bridge the gaps, add value and get stuff done. It's because of cross-functional collaboration that work happens, that connections, barriers, or breaks get identified, and that collective success is possible. Being able to effectively navigate the distance between different teams and disciplines, as well as find the commonalities to move quickly and productively through problems and toward big picture goals, is helpful for the candidates and hiring team alike.

Because of these factors, the cross-functional team member may serve as an astute judge for a specific set of your skills and capabilities, or might provide a more general read on how they believe you will collaborate, communicate, and contribute to relevant initiatives.

In an ideal world, the cross-functional conversations expand your understanding of the business, projects, and team dynamics and give you a more well-rounded view into the overall organization as well as how it operates day-to-day. Like a peer, cross-functional interviewers are often eager to find a strong, skilled hire and will spend the extra time in interviews and follow-up conversations to support that outcome. There will be occasions, however, where internal tensions, existing friction around project goals or ownership, in addition to interpersonal conflicts, will factor into their interview approach and decision-making process.

During your conversation, focus on the aspects of the broader, matrixed elements of the role that the cross-functional team member is best positioned to answer. Their view from the outside (at least of the specific team you'd be joining) will be different than what you've heard and learned from those interviewers you'd work with directly. It's a great opportunity to listen for the differences and work to understand the underlying reasoning for the various points of view—are the gaps manageable or do you think there are fundamental issues with how each group views a particular situation? These new perspectives provided should help you uncover meaning, recognize additional opportunities for you to build strong relationships and contribute toward key initiatives, and connect dots between the bullets in the job description, the conversations you've had and your own skills and capabilities.

4.9 *Human Resources (HR)*

Put simply, HR helps shape the employee experience via compensation, benefits and administration, talent development and training, and cultural programs, and are called upon to solve other people's problems. They aim to design with all team members in mind while keeping an eye out for consistency, fairness, and legal requirements, balancing their responsibility to the company and its employees.

Depending on the environment and your own experience, HR might be a team that you trust and value and that you see as a partner and advisor, or you may view them as a cumbersome administrative function that complicates what should be simple and reduces what is actually complex to an annoying form or checklist. In fact, these are two of the more positive views into the role that HR plays in organizations. In some companies, and for many people, HR enforces outdated policies and the law, serves to protect the company rather than support the employees, and caters to those who do wrong rather than those who have been wronged. Pair that with the perception that HR doesn't have a real seat at the table, takes a resource-focused versus human-oriented approach to problem solving, and fails to innovate or adapt to an ever-changing workplace—it's not surprising that seeing a HR team member on your interview list may not excite you.

As someone who has had roles within this function in startups and established companies, I've seen the positive and negative impacts of what these teams and individuals can do. I often talk about how I think the function is desperately in need of dramatic change and do my best to support innovation and the infusion of new ideas as part of this transformation. 2020, and the layered impacts of a pandemic with its health and remote work implications (childcare, technology, and more!), reckoning with racial injustice, and layoffs, furloughs, and economic recession have further tested the HR function. With these acknowledgments and my personal beliefs, and despite my passion and intentions, I know I have also missed team members' expectations before. I see these challenges and look back on my own experiences as an ever-present chance to learn more, do more, and grow in my expertise and capabilities. I, like many HR professionals, come into the function because they care about making the work experience better and want to do it for people, with people. Sometimes broader company policies, hierarchy, access to information, or legal requirements interfere with HR's ability to take what would be the best, most efficient and practical path. Additionally, an abundance of employee questions and concerns can take up more time than the innovative culture-building activities that may have inspired them to get into the field.

Still, the HR perspective can be incredibly valuable for candidates navigating the interview process—who may become employees adapting to company operations and personalities. They've seen team members at their best—when projects go well or when promotions and raises get announced—and have been present during those tough times too—when conflicts emerge, terminations occur, or issues pop up. Those diverse experiences give them context, insight, and, hopefully, empathy for what any individual or team might be going through.

In an ideal world (and in this case, an aspirational one), HR has the chance to listen to the voices and represent the interests of employees by developing programs that make current employees committed to their roles, and entice others to want to join the team. In reality, their hard work is mostly behind the scenes where it won't be noticed by most people, and they are often caught between groups or individuals trying to interpret motivations and stories to get to the bottom of a particular situation. They are asked to be pragmatic and objective even though they are dealing with reactive, nuanced, and subjective situations.

During your conversation, raise questions that may be of a sensitive nature (for example, those that give a window into your personal life such as a disability requiring accommodations or questions about childcare benefits or leave policies) that you would not be comfortable asking to other interviewers. Push on the aspects of the total rewards (benefits, health care), and programs and talent management strategy (performance reviews, leadership development, and promotion processes). They will often represent the organizational perspective and process with more objectivity than the anecdotal experience, rusty recollections, or personal opinions of others. Take the opportunity to build a relationship with the HR person so that, if someday you have a problem or tricky situation, you'll feel more comfortable approaching them for support.

4.10 *Direct Report*

When you're interviewing for a managerial or leadership position, you'll want to learn about the dynamics of the team situation you'll be stepping into. Early in the process, start to flesh out the overall picture:

- What is the size of the team?
- Who are the team members?
- What are their roles, tenures, and contributions?

Then ensure you have clarity about a few specifics that might not be proactively addressed:

- Why is this role open (did the person who filled it previously quit or get fired)?
- Does the team know the hiring process has been activated? How do they feel about a new manager stepping in?
- How will the team participate in the interview process? If they will not act as interviewers, when will you be able to meet and interact with them prior to making a decision?

It's hard to be a manager, and it's even harder to step into an existing team and take over trying to build a new path forward while dealing with the legacy or baggage of what someone else might have left behind.

Put simply, a direct report is playing the same role you are playing when you're interviewing with the hiring manager during this process. They are trying to determine if you are their person, if you'll coach and support them in their journey in those real, tangible ways and those hard-to-quantify gut instincts. Like you, they are motivated to find the right person. Your direct reports will play a critical role in your work experience—when you have talented high-performers, work is easier, more enjoyable, and productive. You may form long-lasting relationships with these individuals, work with them at other companies, or perhaps work for *them* someday (especially when you work with exceptional people)!

Depending on the individuals, they may have experience working with many managers and will be able to compare and contrast your strengths with those they've known before, or they may have a single point of reference to measure you against. As a result, the interviews could vary significantly from a timid "getting to know you" conversation to a critical assessment of your capabilities, personality, and leadership style.

In an ideal world, you'll have had several previous conversations with the hiring manager, recruiter, and perhaps the department executive, and will be able to ask questions about the team as a whole as well as the individuals. Make sure you proactively push to get information about the team in these conversations as the interviewers' inclination will likely be to continue to assess you. In some companies, the direct reports are active participants in the process and members of the decision-making team. Other organizations might approach it differently, a smaller group of decision-makers might assess candidates and then introduce direct reports at the final stages with the context of community building rather than evaluation.

◇ IMPORTANT Sometimes, companies won't involve direct reports at all. It's highly important that you meet with your direct reports prior to accepting a position. Early in the process, there may be a need for confidentiality for a number of completely valid reasons, but because the working relationship of a manager to their team is so vital to the health, engagement, and success of the overall group, building those connections as soon as possible and being able to factor those learnings into your ongoing assessment of the opportunity is key. If they do not offer you the chance to meet with a minimum of a couple members of your prospective team, ask directly to do so in the later stages of the process.

⚠ DANGER Should a company deny you the chance to meet with critical team members, including direct reports, before you accept a position, consider it a warning sign that something important isn't being disclosed.

During your conversation, focus on building rapport and capturing details about what matters to them. Be humble and willing to answer any question they ask and try to do it genuinely and with the details that will help them gain confidence and trust in you as a leader. Open the door for them to ask you questions that put you in a vulnerable place—in this conversation it's not about asserting everything you can do and do better than others, but rather understanding how you would step into the team and help everyone reach their individual and collective goals. When you have the floor, ask questions about their motivations, career aspirations, and learning styles, as well as specifics about the projects or work to be done. Talk about feedback styles and preferences and get their insight on bigger picture topics as well—team members from every position in the organization can have incredible insights on interpersonal dynamics and strategic priorities.

4.11 *Back-Channel*

4.11.1 HOW COMPANIES LEARN ABOUT YOU OUTSIDE THE INTERVIEW PROCESS

The concept of a back-channel may or may not be as familiar depending on how often you've been part of interview teams or interviewed yourself.

Put simply, "back-channel" refers to the conversations prospective employers might have with people who know or have worked with you that you have not proactively shared as references. These conversations can happen at any stage of the hiring process, from before they get on the phone to after an offer has been extended. Often companies take this approach to get the "real" story about you, as your official references are most certainly enthusiastic champions—and prepared ones at that! Like references, back-channel conversations are most often used to complement and validate existing beliefs about a particular candidate (mostly positive) and rarely change the course of the process entirely (though, it can happen) so don't *beware* these conversations, but be aware that they might occur.

Not all companies will conduct back-channel references, but you can plan on it by reaching out to mutual connections between you and your interviewers that you discover via LinkedIn to give them a heads up you're interviewing and might hear from the company. This is a good place to remind you that the world is small and people have a tendency to boomerang back into our lives at unexpected points in time. It's not always easy, but it's worth trying to preserve positive relationships and avoid burning too many bridges too spectacularly throughout your career (even if you don't like working with everyone or have some tough relationships) as you never know if one of those individuals will be brought into a conversation about you at some point in the future.

People often worry, sometimes for good reason, about confidentiality when it comes to going public about their job search. If you have significant concerns around this, it's best to be transparent with your recruiter or the hiring manager up front about the nature of those concerns and ask that they connect with you before engaging references of any sort. It's not a guarantee, but can prevent awkward conversations, especially if there is a single individual or shortlist of people you'd want to touch base with before they found out you were interviewing. At the same time, interviewing is a common experience and most interviewers and references treat it with a level of respect for candidates' privacy, recognizing how they would like to be treated if they were interviewing.

4.11.2 HOW YOU CAN LEARN MORE ABOUT THE COMPANY OUTSIDE THE INTERVIEW PROCESS

There's another back-channel route to consider—how you can seek back-channel "interviews" about the company or others you meet and might potentially work with. You can take a similar approach to the playbook that they are probably following. In anticipation of your interviews with team members, take time to connect with them on LinkedIn, Twitter, or other social sites and look for common or close connections from work or academic experiences, and also professional organizations and volunteer commitments. If you find someone that you'd feel comfortable speaking with and whom you believe would have valuable, trust-worthy insights, feedback, or resources that could aid in your decision-making, then consider sending a quick note.

In most situations, when you reach out, you can preface the confidential (or at least non-public) context of your interview process and ask if they'd be open to answering some of your questions or sharing some of their experience with the company or with one of the people you'd be working with should you take the job. In an ideal world, they'll take some time to talk through your questions, excitement, and hesitations and provide a more objective point of view than you or the interviewers may be able to given your proximity to the process.

Before you start asking questions, make sure you include some background on why you're searching, what you're optimizing for and prioritizing in a new role and company, and a bit about the process you've gone through so far. That information will help them understand where you're at and tailor their advice accordingly. Having back-channel conversations is not a requirement! But it can be a beneficial exercise. When making a decision that will impact your career and life, there's no harm in asking more questions!

5 Ask Me This Instead

Imagine wrapping up final interviews with a company knowing that you not only had the chance to share your story and skills, but that you gathered all the information you could about the company, team, and role in order to understand whether this is the right opportunity for you. Asking focused questions connected to your personal priorities is empowering and builds your confidence at each step of the process, especially when you need to determine whether to accept an offer.

If you want that feeling, it's time to design a 360° strategy for your interviews. Building your plan will enable you to get the most out of the process, just like structured interviews help interviewers achieve their objectives. Asking targeted questions around your priorities to specific people will make the conversations more illuminating and productive. And, candidates who ask the best questions stand out.

This section of the book exists to help you create the plan and take action to make your interviews work for you. As you dig into the question database, you'll find a common question paired with insights about why it will not get you the information you need. Each of the common questions is then reframed with what you can ask instead, and highlights about why that framing will unlock valuable details about the role, team, and company. This is a chance to bring your voice and power into the process and builds upon the content and exercises from the previous sections of the book. I have aligned questions by persona and topic as a starting point. I encourage you to think about what questions you need to ask and who is the right person for you to ask them to—you may align the questions differently!

5.1 *Ask Me This Instead Question Database*

This section is available in the digital edition at Holloway.com.

5.2 *Activity: Build Your 360° Interview Plan*

> Find the activity in this Google Doc![24]

6 Warning Signs in Interviews

As you progress through the interview process, you'll get unique thoughts and opinions about aspects of the role, its purpose, and what the person who will step into the position will be responsible for achieving from each interviewer. If the interviewers are in general alignment—that is, they have a defined set of clear talking points and their answers are complementary rather than tangential—that's great! You will be able to focus on resolving the differences around the edges or get valuable insight into where potential friction or disagreement might emerge should you join the team.

Unfortunately, not every interview team is aligned. While it may be hard to get visibility as an outsider looking in, if you're aware of some of the dynamics that interviewers may be dealing with among themselves or within the organization, you can pick up on clues to read the room and identify warning signs more effectively. As you go through each conversation, take in the information provided by each interviewer as well as your gut reaction to what you're observing and learning. These tangible insights and instincts can help drive your lines of questioning as you progress, or influence your decision to continue in the interview process or bow out.

6.1 *Is the Hiring Team in Agreement on Why the Role Is Open?*

A role often gets posted when someone who has been doing that work leaves, when a new initiative is launched or when there is a gap or pain point that needs to be addressed and no one internally has the ability or capacity to solve it effectively. There are other reasons why new roles come into being, but those are by far the most frequent.

---

24. https://www.holloway.com/amti-worksheet

In early conversations with the recruiter and hiring manager, ask questions to understand why this position is open. As you continue through the interview process, pay attention to what other team members share to see if they continue to reinforce or contradict what you've already heard. Gaps in alignment may seem inconsequential. However, they have the potential to grow and complicate working relationships and outcomes over time. Understanding if everyone agrees on the need for the role and how the position's responsibilities will be integrated to complement and strengthen existing efforts is key.

⚠ DANGER Warning Signs!

- **It appears that the team is solving for pain, rather than hiring with a plan.** Are interviewers extremely eager to bring someone on and capable of listing all kinds of issues but light on details around specific responsibilities, timelines, or milestones? This may be a sign that they know they have a problem, but aren't quite aligned on the appropriate plan or hire to address the issues.
- **Communication is inconsistent, inaccurate, or absent.** Communication challenges might be between hiring team members as well as with you, leaving you wondering what's next, what happened, and what does it all mean.
- **An interviewer makes remarks or downplays the role or the contributions associated with it.** An existing team member may be currently fulfilling some of these responsibilities and could be hesitant to let them go. They may also have a different perspective on how the role or work should be structured.

6.2 *Is There Clarity on the Responsibilities for the Role?*

For there to be clarity on responsibilities, whether a backfill or new position, the hiring manager would need to assess relevant changes to the business and how those might impact the profile of talent, goals, or requirements associated with the position. It's the combination of reflection, forward-thinking evaluation and effective communication to the hiring team that will lead to a consistent view into the role and set an interview process up for success. To do this requires extra work. Often, the hiring manager doesn't have the ability to reflect and assess thoroughly so the burden to connect what you are seeing and hearing is your responsibility.

⚠ DANGER Warning Signs!

- **The way the interviewers describe the work does not align with what is outlined in the job description.** Do the interviews add new responsibilities into the mix or talk about an entirely different type of work? It's possible that, depending on their own role, people will highlight and focus on different things so be cognizant of the nature and significance of the gaps.
- **Signs of confusion or misalignment with ownership or execution responsibilities connected to the position.** Do different interviewers share contrary information about how the work will be done or who will be driving specific activities?
- **The interview process design or execution seems haphazard.** Is there a clear and organized approach to the interview process to screen for the capabilities that a new hire will need in order to be successful? Do your conversations seem redundant, or does each interview increase your knowledge and understanding of the role and how you'd contribute?

6.3 *Is the Hiring Team Invested in Your Success?*

Often the person writing the job description and crafting the expectations has a credible understanding of what needs to be done, the skills required, and how the role fits into the broader context or team. Perhaps they have done similar work themselves or managed a team with similar positions and goals. If this is the case for the role you're interviewing for, it will be to your advantage. However, it is possible that the hiring manager is scoping a role that is distant from their own expertise and experience. In this scenario, there is a chance that, despite their best intentions, they miss the mark on defining the work and aligning the requirements to specific skills, capabilities, and knowledge and may not be as targeted or effective in screening candidates at every stage of the interview process.

⚠ DANGER Warning Signs!

- **There is a significant disconnect between the title and responsibilities.** For example, they are hiring a "Director," but the responsibilities represent those typically fulfilled by entry-level positions or use terms and descriptions that don't quite align with what you'd expect to see in that position.
- **Interviewers seem unprepared in the conversations.** You might encounter unprepared interviewers, which can be very frustrating when you think it could impact their ability to accurately assess your potential for the role, and especially when you've prepared.. The lack of preparation could be apparent with any interviewer, regardless of their level or role in the hiring process, and could be due to a lack of clarity about the role, an absence of interview structure and guidance, process fatigue (i.e. having interviewed many candidates in quick succession or as a result of a long, drawn-out process) or the reality that a busy calendar or urgent issue limited their ability to adequately prepare.
- **The hiring manager has followed a very different career path and is new to managing people in this discipline/domain.** This can be an opportunity and a challenge depending on what you are looking for in a manager. If you want to be autonomous, it could be an advantage, if you are confident in their ability to listen, understand, and support or advocate for what you need.

- **The hiring manager and interview team have little to share about the onboarding process.** Depending on the company stage and internal processes in place, there may be robust planning and coordination or a bare-bones approach. The most important thing is to understand if the team is thinking beyond the interviews and how much of a role you'll have to play in structuring or supporting your own onboarding process.

Any of these warning signs, along with anything else that gives you pause, might impact your interviewing experience. You are not able to control or change the experience in many cases, which can be frustrating. If you encounter any of these warning signs, it is worthwhile to reconnect with the hiring manager or recruiter. Approach the conversation in a positive and proactive way, using exploratory questions like the ones outlined in the Ask Me This Instead question database.§5

7 Developmental Career Strategy

By this point, you've put in a tremendous amount of thought and preparation into getting the best outcome from the interview process, which gives you a meaningful advantage relative to other candidates. You have done more in that effort than the large majority of candidates ever will, and you'll be better off in your next job and throughout your career because of it.

Hiring is hard and companies have an advantage. They know the pool of candidates they are working with, they can click through resumes, peruse LinkedIn, and control the flow of the process while they decide who is the "best." They have the chance to test, compare, and see how everything settles. Hiring teams get to ask, ask, and ask some more. Then, at some point, they make a decision. If it's an offer, they push, nudge, and smile to get you to accept and join on their timeline, and with their terms.

Companies often talk about hiring the "best people." Realistically, teams hire the right person to do the work well enough, and who is also interested, available, and known to the company. I realize this is less impressive from an ego perspective and less punchy as an employment brand headline, but it's closer to the truth. Someone can be the right hire in one environment—succeeding, thriving, and delivering impact all day, every day—and fail in another environment. It's the mutual match that matters.

◇ **IMPORTANT** If you put the practices outlined in this book to use continually, you'll have an even greater advantage. You will:

- Find and evaluate career opportunities as they arise.
- Learn about different companies and industries, meet people from various teams, and match roles with your priorities with more confidence.
- Be ready to tell your story, advocate for what matters, and succeed in navigating the hiring process.
- *Be empowered to choose the job you want, not just the job you need.*

7.1 *Take Power in the Process*

Now, I want to remind you of your power in this process so you can seize your potential.

- **When you know and commit to your priorities, you have power.** With reflection and preparation, you're going to hone in on what is most important to you as you go through the job search and interview process. Then, when you're in the interview room, you can focus on being authentically you. If you feel yourself putting on an act, projecting something that is not naturally you, or compromising on one of your priorities, beware! Think of the effort it'll take to sustain and maintain energy, engagement, and commitment to the work if you've made compromises on the things that matter most.
- **When you have a plan, you have power.** You might have wondered while reading why you should take all these steps to prepare for your interviews and might still be doubtful about your intent to follow through. Having a plan gives you power; you aren't only subject to the company's process but can take steps to ensure that your priorities are covered as well. When you walk in with a plan, you can maximize the limited amount of time you have with each interviewer and target your follow-up on the most important items. Getting to interview for a job you're really excited about is hard enough. If you don't know what you want out of the process, you'll miss the opportunity to get the job that could be right for you.

- **When you are proactive, you have power.** Knowing what is most important to you, asserting your preferences, and collaborating throughout the process (interviews are a mutual exercise!) is empowering. By asking targeted questions, you'll demonstrate your capabilities and confidence far more effectively than providing polite, respectful, diplomatic answers. Both the company and you want the best outcome—a strong mutual match based on known strengths and acceptable tradeoffs. If someone pushes back when you ask questions to get the answers you need, think about whether this is the kind of place you'd be inspired to do your best work.

7.2 *Nurture Your Network*

You should start looking for a job long before you're ready to apply or make the move. This is the interviewing equivalent of "always be closing." You should "always be looking." To do this successfully, you need to find credible websites that focus on the roles and companies that are most in line with your interests (for example, B Work[25] for mission-driven job seekers, Jopwell[26] for Black, Latinx, and Native American students and professionals, or FlexJobs[27] for remote or work-from-home roles). To find these niche boards, pair a role or function, for example "design" with the words "job board" and you'll quickly discover sites like Dribbble[28] or Behance.[29] These are not the big job search engine sites. Those sites, including LinkedIn or Indeed, can be helpful when you know precisely what you're searching for and want to see what openings might be available within your geographic area or search criteria. Next, you should subscribe to newsletters or updates that you can consume on your own timeline (or when an interesting subject line catches your eye) and that include reliable highlights about leaders challenging the status quo, companies making a difference, or products that are changing the way people perceive, experience, or spend their money within a particular space.

---

25. https://www.bwork.com/
26. https://www.jopwell.com/jobs
27. https://www.flexjobs.com/jobs
28. https://dribbble.com/jobs
29. https://www.behance.net/joblist

Even if you do not want to have a prolific voice on social media, establishing a presence by following interesting people who comment on relevant topics, have roles that you'd aspire to have or who surface articles, podcasts, or posts that intrigue you is beneficial. "Using Twitter,"[30] by Fadeke Adegbuyi provides expert advice on how to use Twitter to find a job (including those that are never posted!), build your network, and advance your career. This is important to start and sustain before you need a job, you never know when you might hear or find something worth pursuing!

◇ **IMPORTANT** You should also cultivate and invest in your network on an ongoing basis. Your LinkedIn connections are only valuable if you can activate them (i.e. get a response when you reach out)! One strategy is to organize your connections into three groups.

1. Connections you *need* to stay in touch with—these are the individuals who have made a difference in your career, with whom you'd gladly work again, people you could ask to be a reference, or who you believe will play an important ongoing role in your career. This group is probably 15–20% of your network.

   - Make a plan to reach out to these individuals 2–3 times a year if you're not actively working with them. I block time at a couple intervals throughout the year to actively touch base with this group within my network. One of my touchpoints is a personal email or LinkedIn message and then I try to text, comment on a milestone post, or get together in person (outside of a pandemic) for another touchpoint.

2. Connections you *want* to stay in touch with or build a relationship with—these are individuals who are not as close as those in the group above but who might work in a similar role or field or at a company you find interesting, or individuals who you'd feel comfortable reaching out to if you were looking for advice or a new role. This group likely represents about 25% of your network.

---

30. https://www.holloway.com/g/using-twitter

- Check in with this group at least once a year via a personal email, LinkedIn message, text, or a coffee meetup. This group has the potential to point you toward interesting opportunities you would otherwise not hear about!

3. Other connections—these are individuals who you may have crossed paths with directly or who are in your network due to common connections, interesting posts, or quite possibly for some unknown reason! You may or may not have ever had a direct interaction. While it's possible that these individuals could play an active role in your career, it's unlikely. This group could represent 50% or more of your network.

   - Respond to requests that seem viable or interesting and comment, share, or like their posts if it makes sense.

Keep a pulse on what or who piques your interest consistently from the activities above. It's possible that you will find a single, amazing opportunity that you'll be able to pursue and everything will come together. Those rare instances where serendipity and the forces of the world converge can happen, and it's exciting when they do. More often, it's a process. You'll follow people and companies or search for a category or two of roles and start to get a feeling for how particular companies and teams represent their opportunities. When you first start searching, you might have a pretty narrow set of criteria that you're focusing on. As you progress, it will likely expand, and then, with many examples as a reference, you can begin to calibrate, see through the marketing (and occasional false advertising), to refine your efforts again in a more targeted direction.

7.3 *Interview, Interview, Interview*

You build on your power and seize your potential when you *interview every chance you get*. To the job of your dreams, you have to show up at your best. You don't show up at your best without practicing. I want you to interview every chance you get, or at least every year.

◇ IMPORTANT **Why should you look elsewhere when you have a job you like?** It's the best way to make sure you are there for the right reasons—engaged, enthusiastic, and all-in. Thinking clearly about your career path and preparing to succeed in interviews is more easily approached when you're not under the pressure of needing a new pay-check, and when you have the chance to weigh your current role's pros and cons relative to any move you'd consider making. This provocative approach to interviewing opens the door for honest reflection throughout your career. It gives you the freedom to see what else is out there and determine if what you have is better than other options available. You can explore and have conversations to learn more about yourself and how a role and company can support your interests and priorities. It also helps you understand how your experience and skills are valued in the market-place, which can help you negotiate an offer or go back to your company and ask for a raise. These realizations unlock something powerful—you have options.

If you keep your skills fresh, do your best in the role and cultivate relationships with current, former, and prospective colleagues, you won't be stuck. So, even when you love your job, answer recruiters' emails and apply for jobs that look amazing. Sometimes these efforts will go nowhere. Other times, they'll yield worthwhile conversations and new insights. And maybe, they'll end up pointing you to the next best opportunity for you—one that you wouldn't have found without looking at your career as a journey with multiple destinations and a variety of ways to get from here to there.

You will learn every time you go through the interview process as you reflect on the work you've done and what you've achieved or messed up. You get to articulate your story, refine your value proposition, and learn about yourself and a bit of the world beyond. Maybe the conversations you have this year aren't the ones that lead you to make a shift, but they help ensure you're ready and prepared if and when that right role comes becomes a real possibility.

7.4 *Get Ready to Run*

So how do you know if you've found the "one"—the job that's right for you, right now? You should answer one of my favorite questions to ask candidates for yourself. I like to close final round interviews by asking, "*What would make you run toward this opportunity with enthusiasm and what would make you run away?*"

I give this advice because, though I have asked this exact question dozens of times to others, I didn't ask it to myself a few years ago. While working long hours in a demanding job, I found myself daydreaming about quitting during the day and casually scrolling through job postings or venting about my job to friends in the evenings. Though I couldn't see it and truly didn't realize it, I was already running away. So, when a compelling opportunity with awesome people came up, I took it. It was, objectively, a great job, but it wasn't the right job for me. Had I taken the time to evaluate my priorities, explore what options were out there—and crucially, had I asked better questions of my interviewers—I could have saved myself and a team I cared about a lot of time, effort and... emotional turmoil. Look, this type of thing happens, and it's not necessarily anyone's fault, but the work and approach outlined in this book can save you and others from having to have the same experience I had.

It is best to intentionally move toward a new role rather than leave a job for *any* role other than your current position. As an interviewer, the "run toward" question gave me some of the best clues and cues about what mattered to the candidate, where their mind was, and what our risks were if we wanted to hire them and bring them onto the team. I knew it was getting at something when I started to see how people reacted to the question. It often made them sit back, smile, and genuinely reflect before they answered.

So think about a job you are interviewing for.

Are you running toward this role? Here are some of the most telling signals:

- You start telling everyone about the company, the role, the people.
- You start using "we" as if you're already part of the team.
- You think about it non-stop, ideas or reflections pop into your mind at unexpected times.
- You start to "do" the work—the questions and problems you've learned about are so interesting that, in your spare time, you begin to research and dig into them to try to solve them.
- Your gut is telling you that these are your people, this company represents your purpose and this product is the one you want to support.
- You realize that if you were to sit down and craft your dream job, it'd look a lot like this one.

Or, are you running away? These might be indicators that you should explore other paths:

- Your conversations leave you with more questions than answers.
- You get an odd feeling about interactions with members of the team—nothing specific but something's still off.
- You get the impression that what the job description or careers site promised is more fiction than truth.
- You are experiencing stress or anxiety even if the process has positive momentum.
- You cry ugly, not happy, tears when you get an offer and don't know what to do (not that this has ever happened to me...)
- You are bored and uninspired during interviews and forget about them the minute you walk out the door.
- You'd be "OK" if it didn't work out.

Finding your place is as much about eliminating the options that won't fulfill your expectations and aspirations as it is about locking in on the ones with the most potential. Going into such a major decision with eyes wide open provides the greatest odds of a beneficial experience and outcome for everyone involved, especially you!

This book is for you. Where are you running to?

About the Author

Kendra Haberkorn has led recruiting, people ops initiatives, and teams at world class consulting firms, large corporations, and fast growing startups. Her passion lies in enabling people to discover and access the career opportunities that will tap into their talents and complement their lives. With experience creating programs that impact the full employee experience, Kendra aims to design for and support mutual success–for the business and for teams and individuals. Based in Denver, Colorado, she works with early to mid-stage startups around the country to build strong people ops and talent functions, hire exceptional team members, and solve cultural, team, and operational challenges through periods of growth and transformation.

About Holloway

Holloway publishes books online, offering titles from experts on topics ranging from tools and technology to teamwork and entrepreneurship. All titles are built for a satisfying reading experience on the web as well as in print. The Holloway Reader helps readers find what they need in search results, and permits authors and editors to make ongoing improvements.

Holloway seeks to publish more exceptional authors. We believe that a new company with modern tools can make publishing a better experience for authors and help them reach their audience. If you're a writer with a manuscript or idea, please get in touch at hello@holloway.com.